ACCLAIM FOR

WIN THE 16

"Wonderfully uplifting and practical wisdom from a first-time author. Weaving in entertaining anecdotes and stories. Dave Pygon brings the wealth of his lengthy business career to life with a very personal touch! As a very busy spine surgeon and businessman, I can honestly say his *"Win the 16"*, as outlined in this book and illustrated in his podcast, has been enlightening, easy to implement, and most importantly, very effective for me personally and professionally!"

- **Dante Implicito, M.D., Section Chief, Spinal Surgery Hackensack University Medical Center, President and CEO, DocSecure Insurance Company**

"If you're wondering what differentiates highly successful people and would like to improve your daily impact, this book is a must read. *Win the 16* is practical, insightful, action-oriented, and full of distilled wisdom for people at all stages of their career and personal journey."

- **Anthony Wallace, Vice President & General Manager, Bausch + Lomb**

"As a fellow author & small business owner, I easily relate to Dave's journey. In his *Win the 16*, he successfully describes his winning strategy in an impactful book. Dave is winning the 16 and shows how you can too."

- **Jeff Hoffmann, award-winning debut author of "Other People's Children" and Co-Founder of Advanced Information Solutions**

"Having read many leadership books through the years, I found *Win the 16* refreshing and different from many traditional leadership novels. Dave Pygon's effective use of storytelling shares how different leaders inspire others to greatness and helps educate the reader on critical concepts such as inspirational leadership, motivational leadership and goal setting. *Win the 16* is a mindset, philosophy and lifestyle that is well worth the read!"

- **David Mayer, M.D., author of "How to Stay Safe When Entering the Healthcare System", Founding Director Emeritus, MedStar Health Institute for Quality and Safety**

"*Win the 16*", written by Dave Pygon, demonstrates the methods of how to implement the drive, the patience, and the discipline to obtain personal goals. Growing up in our household, I was always reminded that demonstrating a strong work ethic makes people more successful. These are the fundamentals needed to conquer obstacles we may face throughout our lives. A must read for all."

- **Hector Graciano, President and CEO, Electric Motor Services, Inc**

"*Win the 16* is a recipe for success. Dave takes you step-by-step, chapter by chapter, on what to do to achieve a healthy successful life. The small steps we repeat every day create habits that can improve our lives. These steps can be applied to our careers, health and relationships. A great read for anyone looking to succeed."

- **Mary Ryan, Vice President, Miken Cartage, Inc**

"*Win the 16* offers numerous strategies to simplify and improve one's life and work while emphasizing the importance of reflection, motivation, and inspiration in achieving one's goals. Dave argues that anyone can be inspirational and encourages readers to make the most of their 16 waking hours by embracing a mindset, lifestyle, and philosophy that promotes deep thinking and personal growth. As a former Notre Dame football player and current technology business owner, I can tell you the topics and lessons covered in this book will help you become a high performer in anything you do."

- **Nic Weishar, Co-Founder & Head of Finance, YOKE**

"The beauty behind the *Win the 16* principles are that the teachings are both relevant and implementable for all. I have incorporated aspects into my personal and professional life, and I have recommended *Win the 16* to my children, who are just starting their careers."

- **Shawn O'Neil, Chief Commercial Officer, ViaLase, Inc**

"Dave Pygon's *Win The 16* is the invaluable compass you need to keep the course on your goal-reaching journey. By adopting its impactful mantra, *Win The 16* reshapes the hopeful idea of becoming your best-self into a strategic plan. His lessons will not only teach you how to optimize and conquer every waking hour of the day, but they'll serve as the crutch you can lean on when motivation isn't enough. A must-read for those looking to steer clear of complacency and level-up mentally, physically, and professionally."

- **Nick Rella Jr, Enterprise Relationship Manager, Bloomberg LP**

"Whether you are the leader of a major corporation, the head coach of a local sports team, or an individual contributor at a start-up, *Win the 16* has lessons for all. The principles outlined in *Win the 16* provide a clear road map for successfully maximizing our potential every day."

- **Christian Doucet, Owner, All Dry Services of Fort Worth, TX**

"Whether you are an individual contributor or leader, *Win the 16* embodies the habits and attributes needed to achieve success and get to your goals. This book is practical, and each chapter has nuggets of useful information you can immediately apply to your personal and professional lives. Dave is a great storyteller and provides real-world examples. *Win the 16* is a valuable resource for anyone looking to improve and get better."

- **Paul Rosen, Chief Revenue Officer, ShipBob, Inc**

"Dave Pygon, my former high school basketball teammate at St. Rita, captures the essence of developing every day with *Win the 16*. This is a must read for anyone who is looking to improve in life."

- **Curtis Price, Athletic Director, Chicago St. Rita High School**

"*Win the 16* is a proven concept. Our Dad has been living this existence our entire lives. No matter your age or occupation, you can learn from this book."

- **Tyler Pygon, Executive Account Manager, CDW**
- **Jason Pygon, Sales Development Representative, YCharts**
- **Jake Pygon, Associate Account Manager, Northern Trust**

WIN THE 16

Principles and Strategies to Optimize Your Day

Dave Pygon

Copyright ©2023 *Dave Pygon*

All Rights Reserved

Special Credit for my Editor:

Susan Strecker

Dedication

To Mom, for emphasizing education, discipline, mental toughness and more in our childhood. This book is not possible without your commitment and dedication to raising three boys on your own. You're the best!

To my brothers, Bud and Brian, you were always role models that were instrumental in my life. God bless Brian, who passed away in 2018. Bud, you continue to inspire and share your expertise as well as learnings, which continue to support me in my journey of life.

To Susan, my wonderful, kind, intelligent and beautiful wife. Thank you for entering my life and making me whole as well as a better human being.

To Tyler, Jake and Jason, you are and will continue to be one of the driving forces in my quest to live until I am one hundred years old. Blessed to have three special sons.

To my inner circle of friends, and you know who you are, thank you for your unconditional friendship, knowledge, kindness, inspiration, and honesty, as well as the love for my entire family, which you are as well.

About the Author

Dave Pygon

EDUCATION:

- Northern Illinois University Graduate 1991 Major Political Science, Minor Economics
- Chicago St. Rita High School

CAREER:

- Automatic Data Processing
- Alcon Laboratories
- Novartis
- Pygon ONE Consulting, President and Owner

CERTIFICATIONS:

- Business Coach
- Behavioral Consultant
- Advanced Behavioral Analysis
- Time Management
- Master Life Coach

EXPERIENCES:

- Over twenty years in leadership
- Created own company, Pygon ONE Consulting
- Author
- Coach

- Consulting background
- Motivational speaking
- C-Suite, training, development, sales, marketing, negotiating, on-boarding and career enhancement
- Business, marketing, sales, budget, operational, and strategic plan
- Organizational restructuring
- Assisted in building multiple new divisions
- Hiring and retaining talent
- Built Podcast "*Win the 16*" and podcast co-host

NOT-FOR-PROFIT:

- Creator and Emeritus President Windy City Magic AAU organization
- Over ten years of "youth" coaching
- Board of Directors: The Care Kit Foundation

CORE VALUES:

- Family, Health, Integrity, Trust and Positivity

Contents

Foreword vi

Introduction x

Chapter 1 - South Side Chicago 1

Chapter 2 - Win the 16 6

Chapter 3 - Motivators 15

Chapter 4 – Inspiration 23

Chapter 5 - Can an optimistic philosophy coexist with being negative at times? 30

Chapter 6 - Positivity 34

Chapter 7 - Mindset 42

Chapter 8 - Mental Toughness 50

Chapter 9 - Early Success in your Day 60

Chapter 10 - Goals 66

Chapter 11 - Habits 73

Chapter 12 - Discipline 79

Chapter 13 – Time Management 85

Chapter 14 - Unforeseen Challenges and Obstacles 92

Chapter 15 - Change Agility 95

Chapter 16 - Healthy Lifestyle 102

Chapter 17 – Coaching 110

Chapter 18 – Accountability 119

Chapter 19 – Happiness and Future 125

Chapter 20 - 960 129

Chapter 21 - Mission Plan 134

Chapter 22 - Your Greatest 365 139

Chapter 23 - Final Thoughts 143

Appreciation 146

About Pygon ONE Consulting 147

Foreword

My earliest memory is my pregnant mom standing on a Black Hills, South Dakota helicopter tarmac. She was told she couldn't go on the helicopter tour of Mount Rushmore with my dad, my brother Brian, and me. I got scared. If the ride isn't safe for my mom, was it safe for me? I spent the ride praying we would be OK. This is where the story begins.

Three months later November 23rd, 1969, Dave was born. Funny. I don't really remember that.

The South Dakota vacation was the first and last we took as a nuclear family. My parents divorced in the fall of 1971 after my dad resigned from his job amid a series of bad decisions he made. The bank foreclosed on our house and my mom, Brian, Dave, and I moved back to Chicago to live with our maternal grandparents in the same south side two-flat that my mom grew up in.

Those first few months were rough. I do remember getting into a lot of fights at school as bullies tested the new kid on the block while I tried to make sense of our new place in life. We were the only kids of divorced parents in a Catholic parish. It was a different, less tolerant time.

My mom was a rock but now worked long hours just to make ends meet. Not easy for a non-college educated woman in the 1970's. My grandparents were our saviors providing room, board, stability, and a lot of unconditional love. It wasn't long before I felt fortunate to be living with my grandparents in Chicago. Our new home was full of love, my grandfather's great stories, and my grandmother's wonderful cooking. In addition, I liked Chicago. Our neighborhood had sports crazed kids like me that were always out playing games. Since Brian, nearly two years younger but always as big as me, was a constant companion, we were almost always welcome in the neighborhood pick-up games. He'd play for one team. I would get picked by the other. Brian was a blessing. Those daily pick-up games were too.

Dave is nearly six years younger than me, but as soon as he could run and ride his bike, he started tagging along with Brian and me. We played sports in the neighborhood every day, rode our bikes to the park, often to play sports, and when it was time to come in, we played board games at neighbor's houses. Dave always pushed himself to keep up even when it was next to impossible. I remember his great spirit and being a willing fill-in whenever he was needed. He was fearless and resilient. He got knocked down a lot but always got up excited for more.

Fast forward a few years, Dave grows into a precocious athlete, can hold his own by around fourth grade, and frankly is better than most of the neighborhood by sixth grade. Given my life consisted of going to school and playing sports, we spent a ton of time together.

The seeds of Win the 16 were planted here. Dave used the physical challenges of playing with older kids to fuel not frustrate him. He patiently waited, sometimes for hours, for a kid to leave the game so he could play. He was disciplined, practiced, and thoughtful. He knew his limitations and played to his strengths. He identified other's weaknesses and calculated how to be his best-self against them. I never remember him getting down, only upbeat with an "I can do it" attitude that was infectious even then. He displayed remarkable maturity and an ability to get along with a diverse group that foreshadowed his sharp emotional intelligence and wonderful relationship skills. My old neighborhood friends still remember and love Dave.

More than three decades later Dave has parlayed his natural talents, hard earned business experiences, an unyielding optimism, and well-honed leadership skills to create Pygon ONE, a consulting company, host Win the 16 podcasts on leadership, and write this book. Win the 16 lays out a road map of how anyone can learn, grow, and explore their potential. He's been living Win the 16 his entire life and this book provides cogent insights on how you can, too.

Dave's been coaching me for years, long before he had his own consulting firm or the catchy name for his lifestyle. Since 2012, the year I remember committing to being different inspired by the adoption of my fourth child, Dave has helped me explore my motivations, set achievable goals, establish habits, improve my time management, and be a supportive accountability partner. In that time, I became the

Chief Medical Officer University of Illinois Health, created enough work-life balance to coach my daughter's sports teams, lose thirty pounds, and complete a Spartan Race with my twenty something nephews. Dave, Thank you. Win the 16 works.

- **Bud Pygon, M.D.**
Senior Associate Head,
Professor of Clinical Anesthesiology,
Past Chief Medical Officer University of Illinois Health

Introduction

People ask, what is *Win the 16*? Is it a motto, product, slogan or service? My response—it's a way of life, mindset, and philosophy. As humans, we have the desire to wake up, enjoy our day and be productive in some capacity. *Win the 16* is a lifestyle and mindset for employees, parents, students, executives, chefs, athletes, business owners, construction workers, educators, caregivers, retirees, and basically all of us on this incredible planet Earth. *Win the 16* refers to the sixteen waking hours we all have if we sleep eight hours a night. It's the 960 minutes available to us to *Win the 16* that day.

This book is practical, with real-world applications and stories to help your days. It's not about every day is going to be wonderful and joyous. The daily journey does have its bumps along the way. This book will deliver real strategies and principles to help us in our daily lives. *Win the 16* was created to support us on our expedition, to help us be productive and to handle unforeseen obstacles and the everyday challenges of modern life. It helps us set goals, modify habits, and create new ones to achieve those goals. It can motivate us, establish disciplined behavior guide, and time management. It can assist with developing mental toughness, a healthy lifestyle, a growth mindset, and the accountability we need to achieve the results we crave. At the end of the day, if we can be proud of our actions, accomplishments, and management of our daily obstacles, we can proclaim we won the 16 that day.

How was *Win the 16* created? For years, I would text family members and say, enjoy your day and win it. A couple of years ago, my brother and I bought our family shirts with inspirational words to win the day. When I started thinking about building a curriculum for my consulting company, I deliberated on the concept of 'how can we be our best selves'. Sleep is important to being our best selves. Experts believe eight hours of sleep is good for us, so I devised *Win the 16* by taking twenty-four hours in a day and then subtracting our eight hours of sleep to arrive at sixteen waking hours to work with to create our own quality-day.

One day, I was speaking to my brother, Bud, on this topic, and he told me I'd been living the *Win the 16* lifestyle since I was a kid. He was right! I always woke up early being positive, optimistic and goal-driven ready to attack that day. Those who aren't morning people might not love my early-morning smile and pleasant greeting to the day, but that is who I am. I've always enjoyed early-morning successes such as a workout before the kids wake up or work begins. My mindset is optimistic. I believe things will work out. Norma Pygon, my mom, embedded us with discipline and working hard our entire lives. I hate wasting time, so time management is natural. At work as a leader, I routinely articulate to the team that you want me when times are tough, and things appear bleak. We will stay calm, take a deep breath, THINK first, implement a strategic mindset and do what is best for the situation, which at times isn't always fixing the problem.

It could be to do the best we can handling this difficult moment, so we can put our heads down at night knowing we did whatever is possible to resolve the obstacles. *Win the 16* does not always deliver the outcomes we desire. However, it does give us an excellent opportunity to achieve, though, if we execute and implement these strategies. *Win the* 16 will deliver principles to have a quality day, handle unforeseen challenges, support a strong mindset, and help lead a successful life that you can be proud of that day, no matter what occurs.

My mom, two older brothers, grandparents and I grew up in the Marquette Park area and St. Adrian parish in Chicago. My upbringing and experiences growing up there exposed me to loyalty, hard work, mentally tough people, as well as kind and happy people. What I realized in researching and building the *Win the 16* curriculum is that I have been living this *Win the 16* life and applying its principles for years, and my past played a major role.

The hope is after reading this book, you will be armed with numerous strategies and ideas to help you on your journey. *Win the 16* could propel you to more ideas in building your best self. We are all different. Your *Win the 16* will be different than mine and others. The *Win the 16* principles can be executed by all no matter who you are, what you do, your vision for your life and your desires. This book can help support your dreams. These principles can support your personal and professional development. They are practical and doable. I didn't say they are easy, but you can do it.

Winning the sixteen starts as soon as you read this book. For those who are already living this lifestyle, *Win the 16* will bring you some additional ideas to take your journey even higher and remind you how you are crushing the game of life in your *Win the 16*.

Lastly, I am not famous. You'd never recognize me walking down the street. I am the guy next door who has been blessed in many ways and would like to share some ideas on how to *Win the 16*. We all can improve, and *Win the 16* can propel us to new heights.

Chapter 1 -
South Side Chicago

Many people believe how and where they were born and raised influences their lives. The people, experiences, neighborhood, diversity, family setting, schooling, economics, jobs and more all play a role in how we grow up. I agree. Our family grew up on the south side of Chicago in the 1970s and 1980s near 67th and Western. In many ways, life was simpler compared to today.

My life revolved around family, school, sports, friends and being outside at Marquette Park. Dinner was on the table at 5:30 p.m. when Grandpa arrived home from working all day at ComED. Grandma would cook dinner most weeknights while my mom worked and went to night school. Obviously, cell phones were not created yet, so my compass was the streetlights. When the lights went on, it was time to come home at night. Travel to and from grade school and high school was mostly on foot. Also, we rode our bikes to the park, our sports practices and just about everywhere else. The two exceptions were taking the CTA bus on Western Ave. to 79th Street and then picking up another bus to take us to Ford City Mall to see a movie. The other was taking multiple buses to go to White Sox games or Oak Street beach downtown.

Growing up in a two-flat house on the south side was a moment in time I not only cherish but am convinced made me. My mom, two older brothers and I lived on the second floor, my grandparents lived on the first floor, and my aunt lived in the basement. We were so fortunate to always have someone around. I can vividly recall Father's Day and my friends spending the day with their dads while I was home. My mom told me not to call my friends as they were busy with their dads. Even though I sensed that other parents felt sorry for me on that day, I never did, and neither did my mom. I was one of the few kids on the south side who saw their grandparents every day. They were amazing, and I miss them to this day.

Grandma was tough as nails—I know where my mother gets it. Grandpa was tough, too, he just didn't show it very often. When he retired, he drove us everywhere. Most people who didn't know us thought he was our dad. He looked great and was in good shape. He always protected us. We attached a basketball hoop to our garage, and it changed our lives. We lived in the alley playing sports. My brothers and friends would play for hours every day. My best friend, Terry, and I would play up to one hundred points one-on-one as if it meant everything. In fact, it did to us. The times in that alley played a massive part in who I am. *Win the 16* began in that house, alley and neighborhood. I just didn't know it.

My mother's philosophy of raising three boys on the south side of Chicago was to keep us busy! She preached working hard, being a good person, academics and athletics. Being busy taught us responsibility, discipline, accountability, commitment, work ethic, loyalty, and competition. It kept us off the streets and out of trouble. In the old neighborhood, the troublemakers usually kept to themselves when they knew other kids weren't running in that crowd. We had to earn their respect, but once we did, there was an understanding among the groups. We policed ourselves and kept our distance from one another. Occasionally the two groups would clash, but for the most part we learned to live with each other.

When it was almost time for me to go to high school, I had to decide where I wanted to go. Bud and Brian took the bus twenty-five minutes to Mt. Carmel every day. I loved going there to watch Bud's basketball games. He was a terrific player, and the teams were good. As a thirteen-year-old who loved sports, it was always an exhilarating Friday night to go watch Bud and Mt. Carmel.

Now my decision was on the horizon, which was, do I attend Mt. Carmel? It came down to two schools one month prior to taking the entrance exam. After much deliberation, I decided to attend Chicago St. Rita, even though it was Carmel's biggest rival. It was like Carmel, with its focus on academics, discipline and athletics. The Rita versus Carmel choice was a major decision and ended up being a wonderful one. In 2010 ESPN listed St. Rita versus Mt. Carmel as the biggest rivalry in Illinois. My brothers supported my choice, and we had fun bantering about the rivalry.

After graduating from Northern Illinois University in 1991, I came home and lived with my mom. It wasn't in our old two-flat. She and Grandma had recently moved to a small southside suburb, where my mom still resides. The old neighborhood just couldn't meet the needs of the family at that point, so it was a necessary decision by my mom to leave after so many incredible years and memories in that house.

My oldest brother, Dr. Bud Pygon, who prefers to be called Bud if you meet him, made a comment when we were discussing concepts such as optimizing your day, winning the day, succeeding in the twenty-four hours you have and more. We were getting granular about the principles and strategies of *Win the 16*. He said it was only natural that I cultivate the idea because, from his perspective, I'd been living *Win the 16* since we were kids. I was flabbergasted. But he was right. My start in living *Win the 16* started on the south side in our two-floor flat. I just didn't realize it until Bud pointed it out.

I work daily on the principles of *Win the 16*. I have misses and failures in my daily, weekly and monthly expeditions, just like others. With that said, it's a way of life for me, and I believe in it. This is why this chapter is devoted to the south side of Chicago as well as a devotion to Brian, my other brother. He passed away on September 3rd, 2018, at his home in Salem, Oregon. Brian was unique, eccentric and wonderful. Using the words, one of a kind does not do him justice. Everyone loved the big six-foot-six man. Brian had a unique way of connecting with all.

One of the principles in *Win the 16* that he lived by was the determination to achieve a goal. He was obsessed with becoming a great golfer. He parked his car outside a golf course at midnight with his headlights on to allow himself additional practice time for his putting. He wasn't very good at golf in his early twenties, but he turned himself into a scratch golfer, winning amateur and club events as well as numerous outings. He never stopped improving himself and his game. He died way too early. Brian was special. I wish he were here to tell him that. In his own way, he lived to *Win the 16* when it came to golf. We should all use this program the way my brother did—to help us achieve what's important to us.

Takeaways from this chapter include the following:

- Where we grow up and the experiences, we have impact us

- Family and friends are important in the journey of life

- Reflecting on the past can help us now

- Life has become more complicated and complex

- *Win the 16* strategies can impact all our lives

Chapter 2 - Win the 16

Win the 16 is an inspirational and strategic way to live your daily life. I have pieced together its concepts and principles to create an innovative but achievable program at Pygon ONE Consulting to help people and companies explore their daily potential. The program is designed to help people on their daily journey with guided principles and strategies. On the surface, it might not seem to be novel, but when you really dig into the principles and understand them, it is complex and takes discipline and commitment. It's not easy. But it can be done. You can implement one principle or two or all, and you will make changes on your daily journey, which will lead to dramatic results.

Win the 16 is meant for everyone, including business professionals, parents, coaches, lawyers, plumbers, farmers, cooks, leaders, nurses, high school and college students, athletes, security-guard, teachers, construction workers, engineers, owners, employees, doctors, accountants, retirees, fireman, policemen, military, and more.

Pygon ONE Consulting's formal definition of *Win the 16* is the following:

> *Each day, we are given sixteen waking hours to conquer. Win the 16 means taking full advantage of those hours. It means embracing discipline and making*

choices to achieve victories, no matter how small, throughout the day. Winning is a habit, and successes early in the day can cascade into further successes. Failure and unforeseen moments are sure to happen, but winning the sixteen means course correcting and adjusting our mindset to optimize the moment, be our best selves and finish the day proud.

Win the 16 is a mindset, philosophy and lifestyle. Earlier in the book, I related how my brother, Bud, witnessed how I was already living this lifestyle in my teens. I wish I'd realized it, too, so I could have dug deeper to maximize the opportunities in front of me during my daily life. The strategies and principles of *Win the 16* are the following:

Motivators, inspiration, early successes in your day, mindset, positivity, mental toughness, goals, habits, discipline, time management, change agility, unforeseen challenges and obstacles, healthy living, coaches, accountability and happiness.

Many *Win the 16* principles I exhibited early on in my adulthood were only surface-deep. As I have matured and become wiser, I have been able to dig deeper into the complexity of these strategies to maximize the level of understanding as well as usage of these principles. I wish I knew then what I know now. Let me be clear, I am not perfect and continue to be a work in progress. I have struggles depending on the day, like everyone. I don't lose sight of the concepts, and when I fall short, I am to the point now that I know I was off, declare a miss and redouble my efforts the next day. I continue to stay committed and focused on implementing these principles to explore my potential and my *Win the 16*.

One thing *Win the 16* is not is a Pollyanna view of the world, life and your day. It is not toxic positivity or asking people to be overly optimistic and believe everything is wonderful. When I introduce *Win the 16* to clients, I open the dialogue with the following belief:

> *"We are in a tough, complex and competitive world. At times, negativity surrounds us, whether it's social media, news, business, TV, peers, competitors, friends, family and more. It's not easy in the world we live in. It's even more of a reason to understand and dig deeper into Win the 16. The principles are to help us in our life no matter our age or situation. I absolutely have bad days, and I have absolutely failed many times in my life. Win the 16 is support, reminds and supplies us with real and tangible strategies and a philosophy that we can incorporate to live the life we desire with a mindset of realism, but also optimism."*

Having two older brothers who were great athletes, I fell in love with sports and basketball. I had an advantage over other kids my age. When my brothers and their friends were short a player, they let me step in. Also, when they didn't need me, I would watch them while I practiced shooting and dribbling. On the nights I didn't get to play, Bud would shoot with me after everyone else went home. This was pivotal to the advantage I had over other kids. My brothers and their friends pushed me and didn't take it easy on me. They made me better. Bud also knew when to push and how far to let it go. He allowed me to struggle against the older kids and knew when to step in and take over. He had a natural gift.

Now fast forward to my senior year in high school at St. Rita. We were fortunate to be a very good team and had one of the best basketball players in the Midwest, Curtis Price. Colleges often came to home games to scout him. This was my third year on varsity. My goal was to play in Division 1 (DI). Prior to the season, Curtis and I went to a FIVE-STAR basketball camp in Pennsylvania. Tons of great players and coaches from all over the country were attending this camp, such as Coach K. from Duke, Dale Brown from LSU, Bob Knight from Indiana and more. I remember calling my brothers and telling them to remember the name of a 6'10" player. He was blocking every shot. He was incredible. He had almost twenty block shots in a game. His name was future professional all-star Alonzo Mourning. He and Rick Fox, future Los Angeles Lakers, were both spectacular players. This camp helped our skills, but also gave us exposure to colleges. Between the camp and my senior year, I was gaining interest from the National Association of Intercollegiate Athletics (NAIA), Division II (DII) and Division III (DIII) schools routinely, plus a couple of Division I (DI) schools with Delaware showing the most interest. By the end of my senior year season, no DI offers came through. I was blessed, though because I did have DII and NAIA schools wanting me to play for them.

After the conclusion of my senior season, I played in a Catholic league all-star game against the East Suburban league. The game was attended by colleges still looking for potential players. Northern Illinois University attended the game that night. They offered me a roster spot on next year's team immediately after the game. I was so excited. Now came the tough part, which was talking to my mom. She wanted me to attend Villanova University for academics and try out for the basketball team as a walk-on. This means you don't have a spot on the roster, and maybe, they take one or two players from the tryout that is open to the entire school. The year was 1987. I share that because, in 1985, Villanova won the Men's Basketball National Championship. I wasn't good enough to play for them, so this wasn't a realistic option. After sleeping on it, I told my mom the next day. She didn't love the decision, but she did support me. Looking back, I give my mom a lot of credit. She guided us but also allowed us to make decisions.

In reflecting back, if I would have documented some of the *Win the 16* principles the summer prior to entering Northern Illinois University, it would have been the following:

- Goal—Play DI Basketball

- Habits—All during high school, I worked hard practicing on my own shooting, dribbling and running. Also, I was lucky one of my best friends, Terry, was an excellent football player, and he inspired me to lift weights routinely.

- Discipline—Checked this off strongly when it came to practicing and working out for hoops

These three principles are critical for *Win the 16*. On the surface, you could surmise I did well in terms of executing *Win the 16*. I had a goal, created habits to reach that goal, and was disciplined in my approach. However, let me share the outcome.

DI basketball can be a grind. I am sure all sports are at that level. We were serious about academics and basketball. A student-athlete is a full-time job and more. A typical day in my freshman year included the following:

- 8:00 a.m. to 12:00 p.m. class

- 12:30 p.m. lunch

- 2:00 p.m. training room to get ankles taped before upperclassmen arrive at 2:30 p.m. (mandatory to tape)

- 3:00 p.m. on the court warming-up before practice begins at 3:15 p.m.

- Practice concludes at 6:00 p.m.

- Dinner with the team at 6:45 p.m.

- Study hall 7:30 p.m. to 9:00 p.m. or 9:30 p.m.

Early on, I was the third-string point guard. I was plugging along, and on a bus ride home from playing the University of Wisconsin, I realized I didn't enjoy the process anymore. It stopped being fun. I decided to stay at NIU and graduate in four years while focusing on school and applying for internships.

After I left the basketball team, I had a lot of free time to work and workout, plus play recreational basketball. In fact, friends and I ended up playing probably six to eight hours of basketball a week. I loved it! We competed and played hard. We were not messing around playing pick-up games. The games were physical and very serious.

I am going to fast forward thirty-four years and share where I failed in one of the *Win the 16* principles when making my college decision. As I reflect, I see that the failure was costly.

It wasn't habits or discipline that was my shortcoming in my later years of high school. I had those skills down well when I was in high school in terms of working on my basketball game. I was blessed and lucky because I enjoyed practices and practicing most of the time. My coach at St. Rita was Jim Prunty. He was good. His practices were lively, kept us moving and allowed us to work on our games. I was blessed to have him. Failure was my goal!

My brother Bud who co-hosts *Win the 16* podcasts with me, said, "Goals can be tricky. You need to really dig down deep to figure out what you genuinely want. It is frequent that people have goals on the periphery. Also, you must really spend time by yourself to think about your goals at times."

Bud is 100 percent correct. I didn't dig deep and think about my authentic true goal as I prepared for college. I just aimlessly said, "I want to play DI basketball." The reality is I just wanted to play basketball because I loved the game. I seldom hated practice or workouts. I enjoyed getting extra work in. My goal should have been to play basketball in college, not to be a DI player. If I had been contemplative, I would have realized that I didn't care what level I played at. I just wanted to play because I loved the sport.

I still love the game. My three sons, Tyler, Jason and Jake, played college basketball. It was wonderful watching them all pursue their goals. I enjoyed every moment of their journey. Hopefully, I was able to support and help them on their path. My experience was a miss and a game-changing decision for me primarily because I didn't dig deeper to identify my ultimate, authentic goal, which honestly was to play basketball because I love it. I am accountable for that, as well, as it's a learning experience for me. Luckily, things still worked out by graduating in four years and completing a couple of business internships in college. Now, my basketball career could have been longer if I would have focused on what I really desired and if I had created the proper process as well as thoughts on my goal. This was a miss on goal setting. My skill, talent and size were suited for DII or NAIA-level basketball, not DI.

Takeaways from this chapter include the following:

- *Win the 16* is a mindset, lifestyle and philosophy

- Principles and strategies are instrumental in winning the sixteen

- Sixteen waking hours in a day to work with

- Alone time to just think is beneficial

- Digging deeper with your thoughts into the principles of *Win the 16* is imperative to optimizing the strategies

- *Win the 16* can impact all our lives

Chapter 3 - Motivators

As a business leader for over twenty years, the words *motivators and motivation* were used frequently by the companies I worked for. I also used them in my own businesses. Prior to starting Pygon ONE Consulting, I worked for Automatic Data Processing (ADP), Alcon Laboratories and Novartis.

My first job out of college was as a salesperson at ADP, a comprehensive global provider of cloud-based human capital management solutions that unites human resources payroll, talent, time, tax and benefits administration and a leader in business outsourcing services, analytics and compliance expertise.

Working for ADP was an incredible experience. The leaders, trainers and my peers taught me so much about the art and science of selling. I firmly believe it is an art. The fundamentals they taught during training and continued to teach every week were outstanding. I didn't realize it then but focusing on development never stopped at ADP. ADP never lost sight of developing people because they always made time for it. Whether it was the weekly training on Tuesdays or the weekly meeting with your manager and mentor, they always were developing you. I was surrounded by some of the most impressive salespeople I have ever been around. Their skills were excellent and top-notch. I will never forget Lou, Chris, Kevin, Mark, Troy, John, Paul, Lisa, Michele, Dave and Tony. I am sure I am leaving out some. My apologies. I'm thankful for the major impact on my professional life they all provided.

Motivation at ADP was unique and a big part of my day-to-day life. The company relied on frequent communication and culture to motivate the employees. They emphasized employee engagement as well as training and development as a tool to motivate people. It was very smart. Keeping everyone engaged was good for everyone, as well as the company's development. ADP used some common motivational techniques:

- Weekly, monthly and annual sales quotas
- Weekly reports on performance
- Monthly and quarterly contests
- Annual presidents club trip with the top performers in the country
- Weekly roll call meeting on Tuesday nights at 5:30 p.m.

ADP also utilized a motivational tool that I found to be unique. Every Tuesday night, the entire sales team of forty-five people would meet at one office. We focused on the following:

- Performance

- Training and Development
- Motivation
- Engagement
- Culture (celebrating the week)

The VP of Sales called out each manager to report total sales for their team that week. We could either report the number of sales we made or pass. But everyone knew that passing meant that we hadn't sold anything that week. It was a point of pride to have something every week. My roommate, Paul, also worked for ADP. We pushed each other to excel. I still believe we need a motivational partner in our personal and professional lives that can help motivate us.

Paul and I were both highly motivated not to have to "pass" during those Tuesday night meetings. Weekly roll calls helped us keep our eye on the target. At times it was tough, but the culture that was set from the top down is what made it work.

The night consisted of training and development where one or two people on the team would conduct a skill set workshop on fundamentals, pearls from a unique deal, sales skills, motivation, competitive intelligence and more. Every Tuesday, we reviewed fundamentals or learned new information. After the roll call and training, the executives took us out to eat and talk. I have fond memories of this. If you had a good week, the quality culture was such that it was common for people to approach you, so they could learn and congratulate you. It didn't matter your experience or position. If you had a tough week and had to pass, many people would be supportive. The bosses and your peers would pat you on the back and encourage you. This night was ADP's commitment to culture, motivation, accountability, development and performance. I look back now, and I respect how they didn't make the night just about performance or just about culture. It was a business meeting, development meeting, culture-inspired meeting, motivational occasion, and an accountability meeting every week. From a leader's perspective, they mastered those Tuesday night meetings.

An individual's motivation can be tricky and complex. Some people don't truly think about their motivators, or they don't truly dig into what really drives them. For our own personal development, ensuring we are true to ourselves with critical thought on our genuine motivations is pivotal. Also, a reminder that motivations can change. As a coach, leader, manager, parent or anyone who is trying to motivate someone, we need to listen and be inquisitive to uncover a person's authentic motivators. This is something that I have learned over time. I had missed this with direct reports. I can remember one example.

As a sales leader, we came out with a new incentive program. I shared it with my team, and then I discussed it with each of them individually to ensure comprehension and to receive feedback. One of my direct reports, Dave, was a competitive individual. He liked to perform. While we were talking about this new compensation plan, he shared a couple of things, and I listened. Then I asked Dave if this new incentive plan was a good motivator. He said that money wasn't his biggest motivator. Eye-opening.

I thought I knew Dave so well. I hired him. We communicated well. I thought I knew his top motivation professionally. He was a family man. We discussed money many times. What a miss on my end! The takeaway is as a leader, and it's critically important to ensure we not only know people's motivators, which takes work and time because we need to dig deep and ask questions but remember motivations of people can change, which I learned. Also, people could share what they think you want to hear. He taught me a lesson that day on motivators that I've never forgotten. Thank you, Dave.

Does everyone believe in motivational speeches, books, and quotes? No, they do not. It's imperative we understand our audience because, for some, we need to explain the why of our motivational tactics to increase buy-in. This is true at home and work. I am blessed at home because my kids are into motivational things. They bought into things such as quotes and shirts we bought the family that said *Rise and Grind,* for example. I personally believe in motivation, motivational talks, books and quotes. I remember the motivational talk the legendary basketball Coach Rick Pitino gave to the Alcon leadership team over ten years ago. Coach Pitino was discussing his book *Success is a Choice.* I agree with Coach that our choices dictate our success or lack of success. I still remember his talk on *TEAM* and what each letter means. The coach also talked about installing confidence in your employees. He discussed how we can inspire confidence, aggressiveness and power in people as well as take it away from them depending on how we lead them. Coach Pitino told a story of one of the greatest college basketball games ever. It was 1992, and Coach Pitino was the head basketball coach at Kentucky University at that time. Kentucky was playing Duke University, another historic and incredible college basketball program. Duke was coached by the legend, Mike Krzyzewski.

This game was played in the East Regional Final to determine a spot in the NCAA tournament Final Four, which means if you lose, your season is over. Both teams were highly ranked. Kentucky was winning by one point with under three seconds left in the game. Duke had to go the full length of the court, ninety-four feet, to score. It was highly improbable. Well, there was a timeout, so both teams were in their respective huddles with their coaches. The huddle was crucial to this outcome, per Coach Pitino.

Both teams take the floor, and Duke throws a pass to the best player, Christian Laettner, on their team. He catches the pass that traveled about eighty-five feet in the air, then turns and shoots it. Yes, it goes in! Duke beats Kentucky and Coach Pitino on a last-second shot. Coach Pitino told us this story for a reason. He said, "I lost this game for the team leaving the huddle at the end of the timeout before Duke made that shot at the buzzer with no time left." The last words he communicated to his players walking on the floor were, "Whatever you do, don't foul them." Coach Pitino said they lost because he took the aggressiveness out of his players. His players played passively and allowed Duke to catch the ball and shoot it, and because they were so worried about not making a mistake, they lost the game.

He attributed that loss to his leadership and coaching. My takeaways from Coach Pitino's motivational speech were many, but I will never forget the point about focusing on not making a mistake. Business and life can't be lived worried about making mistakes, and as a leader, it's imperative we don't spend our time telling people what not to do. We need to motivate and empower our people on what to do. Thank you, Coach Pitino, for that real-life lesson.

Is it realistic to be motivated every day of your life?

This is for you to answer. I can only answer for myself, and I don't think so. In my opinion, motivation can be a roller coaster. When people are motivated, they have a higher tolerance for the effort and pain that can occur during the work that is needed. When motivation declines, people's desire and drive does as well.

How do you then succeed and *Win the 16* on the days that you aren't motivated? When you are not motivated, it's imperative you have daily habits, so you will still do what needs to be done and be disciplined enough to do it. You aren't acting because you are motivated at this point. You are acting because you have created the habits and the discipline to execute even if, at that moment or on that day, you are not motivated. Michael Phelps once asked if people thought it was always fun to swim for many hours a day staring at a black line at the bottom of the pool? Just like everyone, he battled every day through his workouts because of habits and discipline, even when he wasn't motivated.

We must be careful not to rely too heavily on motivations. It's the unicorn who is motivated every day. It's not likely all people will be motivated at the job at hand every day. This is where discipline and habits propel you.

Takeaways from this chapter include the following:

- Organizations have options for motivational techniques for their employees

- Personal motivators can be tricky, so ensuring deep thought on them is imperative

- People's motivators can change, so be inquisitive and ask routinely

- Communicate what you want people to do versus what not to do

- Is it realistic to be motivated every day? Habits and discipline are the fundamentals to survive when motivation is not with us

- *Win the 16* can impact all our lives

Chapter 4 – Inspiration

Would it be easier to *Win the 16* if we were inspired every day? The answer would be yes. Does it always happen? No. At times, we must find our own inspiration. This could be communicating with someone you find inspirational, reading, meditation, or performing a task or act that makes you feel inspired. We have control; we just need to activate it. All of us can inspire others. You don't have to be a teacher, manager or famous person to inspire. I have a friend, Frankie, from the old neighborhood who inspires people. Frankie's older brother, Joey, was one of my best friends since kindergarten, which is how we became friends. Frankie and I have become even closer since Joey passed away in the spring of 2016 from a brain tumor. We spent some sad and grueling days watching Joey's health decline in those last three months. Frankie is a hero! He was there every day for hours. Every time I walked into the care facility; he was at his bedside. Frankie's inspiration to the entire family was amazing.

Frankie is one of the more influential and respected people at the high school where he works, his alma mater, Brother Rice High School in Chicago. Frankie is a building engineer at Br. Rice, which means he does it all. He makes sure that the school is up and running. He gets there early when the snow is coming down. He gets the gym ready for special events. If something breaks down, he fixes it. Problem with the heating, they call him. Frankie's actions and how he performs his role inspires those kids. Also, it is how he relates to them. Do all building engineers promote education and tell the kids to study hard and earn good grades? This is exactly what Frankie does. He is not a teacher by title, but he is inspiring and teaching those kids every day. The football coach even had Frankie speak to the kids before a huge game. You ask Frankie if he likes his job? He would say, "No, I love it!" People inspire others, not titles. I know Frankie enjoys being inspired, but what an honor he should feel that he is the one inspiring. He has a gift and it's delivered daily. In March of 2023, Frankie was recognized with the highest of honor a High School can award. He was elected to the hall-of-fame at Brother Rice, which to no surprise for those of us that know him, it brought him to tears.

Inspiration is what drives us from the inside. It's a purpose and something that moves us internally to act. In training or development sessions, leaders are often asked to articulate the difference between motivation and inspiration. Motivation characterizes why a person acts. It is a driving force behind doing something. Motivation is the process that starts, guides, and maintains goal-oriented behaviors.

In my heart, I believe most generations and most people ultimately would like to be inspired and work for a purpose. Some leaders and business owners have commented on how different it can be to work with or lead Generation Y, or 'millennials' is the term used to describe the generation of people born between 1981 and 1996. Sometimes leaders who are not millennials consider leading or working with certain millennials to be more difficult than engaging baby boomers, the generation of people born between 1946 and 1964, or generation X-ers, the generation of people born between 1965 and 1980. Both generations grew up in an environment where if they were told to go dig a hole, they would go just dig a hole. There was an emphasis on work ethic, respect for authority and just how things were done. In comparison, millennials' idealism surfaces in their need for a sense of purpose, being a part of something, enjoying their work, regular check-ins, and believe in what they are doing.

From my perspective, millennials want to work too, and they just want to work for a purpose, understand the goal and be valued. I do too. I believe they are amazing. They have raised some topics and thoughts that should have been discussed years ago. They aren't motivated by being told to get a good job, just make some money and go type on a computer or dig a hole. They want to be inspired. They want to understand, which is a good thing. The millennials challenge leaders like me to evolve and ensure we are inspiring and creating purpose. The challenge for leaders is that this will take change agility, time, and conscious effort to unlearn how things were done in the past. The younger generations are constantly getting involved in good causes. If we can share with them how our services and products help people and causes, the younger generations are all in and will lead the charge. They want to work for a purpose. This type of work inspires and engages them. Values are important to this group. They will proactively share value with people. The millennials were raised to speak up. They will push for change, which is another trait I respect of them. If a cause is important and change needs to occur, they will push for it.

The ability to inspire and create a purpose for our employees, kids, students, teachers, nurses, construction workers and leaders is possible. It has been going on for years. The goal should be for it to become commonplace everywhere, all the time.

Please allow me to share three inspirational experiences I was involved in from the past.

The first experience, I would like to share is from my junior year in high school. In the second semester, I took a poetry class. None of us wanted to take it, but it was a graduation requirement. Our teacher, Dr. K, was faced with a classroom of boys who didn't understand why they had to take the course and read poems. At best, a few of the kids knew that Emily Dickinson and Robert Frost were famous poets and probably only thought of Shakespeare as a playwright. Dr. K. was consistently voted teacher of the year! His class was the most memorable class I ever took in high school. Why? It is simple inspiration. He inspired us to learn how to read poetry, appreciate it and enjoy it. Most of us enjoyed it so much that we received excellent grades. How did this happen? Dr. K. inspired us. He knew the challenge he faced. He focused on inspiring us to enjoy poetry. He opened the class by playing music.

He used music as a creative tool to teach us poetry and how to read it as well as understand it. It was 1986, and Bruce Springsteen was a megastar. Dr. K. played "Born to Run" and analyzed that song from start to finish. We all learned poetry from "Born to Run". He shared some regular poetry and then brought back music—Simon and Garfunkel's famous song, "I Am a Rock". I remember the symbolism of this song about isolation still today. Dr. K. inspired an entire room of immature kids who didn't want to read poetry. I am writing about him in a book thirty-six years later. I haven't communicated with Dr. K. in probably twenty years, so that speaks volumes about the impact his class had on me. He will somehow get a copy of this book.

My next example is from when I conducted consultative account management work in medical practices. We would work with the entire organization, from C-Suite to the front-desk to nurses, etc. One practice's front-desk team really stood out. They welcomed and treated patients at another level. How they addressed patients, and the care and concern they showed them. It was inspiring to watch them interact. I asked one front-desk person how do you do your job so well? She replied that she treated patients the way she wanted her mom to be treated at the doctor's office. She also said that she was aware that contact with the front-desk staff was the start of the patient experience.

The light bulb went on for me again. These folks took their roles to another level. They were part of the medical experience, not just checking people in. They were part of the team who takes care of patients. I will never forget them.

They are an inspired set of individuals working as a team for a purpose.

The final example comes from my work at Alcon. Alcon brought in their leaders every year for a week on leadership development of some capacity to help us. It was appreciated and respected. They were truly committed to developing their leaders and employees. Dating back to 1999, I was trained on Speed of Trust, IDEO thinking (how to think and create ideas), Zig Ziglar public speaking courses, leadership training, consulting, emotional intelligence, understanding different generations and personalities, developing people short and long-term, strength finders, problem-solving, happiness is an advantage, never split the difference, storytelling, strategic thinking and more. These meetings were always inspiring because it was a commitment by the organization to develop us personally and professionally.

One of the meetings we attended had us working with Habitat for Humanity on building a house for a family. It was inspiring to work with my fellow employees on an amazing project. This could be an opportunity for organizations who desire to inspire employees, whether they are baby boomers, generation X, generation Y, or generation Z (born between 1997 and 2013). We know being involved in such an incredible experience, especially the younger generations who seek out inspiration at work, would respect and appreciate this type of event at work. This would absolutely support a company's commitment to employee engagement, culture and "happiness" at work.

Takeaways from this chapter include the following:

- Inspiration helps us achieve whatever we are attempting to accomplish

- Younger generations are asking us to focus on inspiration and purpose at work

- No one needs a title to be inspirational. All of us can inspire someone

- It takes time and thought to inspire as well as to be inspired

- We need to find inspiration to *Win the 16*. Search for it in your readings, with your friends and peers or something to help inspire you daily

- *Win the 16* can impact all our lives

Chapter 5 -
Can an optimistic philosophy coexist with being negative at times?

The official *Win the 16* program was partly built on the following statement: "We live in a tough, complex and challenging world, and at times, negativity seems to surround us whether it's social media, the news, work, people and more." This statement is especially relevant when implementing a strategy from *Win the 16*. The principles of *Win the 16* were created to support us on our journey. We have goals, wants, and desires and are confronted with tough challenges. Some days are clearly better than others. In our walk of life, good things happen all the time. Unfortunately, bad things happen, too.

Can an optimistic, positive person be negative at times? Yes. In fact, it's healthy, natural and authentic for optimistic people to also experience occasional negativity or sadness when faced with challenging or sad moments. The *Win the 16* lifestyle is not a Pollyanna view of the world, that everything is wonderful, and every hour and day of the week is great. We know that is not how the world is. Life is amazing, but it can also be tough and unfair at times.

Currently, three people in my inner circle are battling health issues. How can anyone not be angry, frustrated and upset when we hear troubling news about people we love? These are real issues. All we can do is be human in these situations and be supportive in whatever way that is optimal for the people involved. There are no correct answers. Just be supportive, knowing that we might not be able to do more.

Is it okay to go negative on less important issues, such as work, in contrast to the health of others, as noted above? Another resounding yes! All of us spend a tremendous amount of time at our jobs. The work environment is not getting easier. It's competitive and complex. Covid changed the world. Remote and hybrid jobs have absolutely changed how people perform their roles, and communicate with their supervisors, direct reports, peers, human resources, clients and more. Some people are thriving and completely support remote work, and others are not. They haven't fully embraced employees not in the office. This has caused some angst in the workforce. We have challenges at work that could cause us to go to a dark place. The key is to be able to move beyond it. We need to be able to get out of it quickly and move to a place that is productive and healthy, so we can optimize our day.

Win the 16 offers strategies to help support us when the pressure at work pushes us to another level, upsets, irritates, or angers us. Again, these are natural emotions. Below are steps to handle these situations:

- Step 1 - Take deep breaths to help clear our minds to, reduce stress and calm our emotions.

- Step 2- Ask questions with the intent to better understand another perspective because we might have a blind spot.

- Step 3 - Remove yourself from the situation temporarily. The situation might not be as bad tomorrow.

- Step 4 - Spend time individually thinking of optimal ways to move forward as well as thinking about anything but this for a couple of hours or even a day.

- Step 5 - Reflect on our own selves and understand how we act when we get irritated. We don't want to contribute to an already non-ideal situation. Personally, I get quiet when irritated. I don't usually want to talk about it, or at least not right away. We are all different.

- Step 6 - Never put anything in writing when upset. Take time to have deep thoughts first on this challenge. Intent versus impact does not always show up well on email. Let me repeat, do not send emails when upset.

- Step 7 - Try not to take the problem home to our families (this is hard because we are human - no on/off switch).

This topic was purposely in its own chapter to ensure it was highlighted. Everyone can have bad days. When our loved ones get sick, it's horrible, sad, and upsetting. When things at work or in our personal lives get off-track, it's okay to be not okay. The key to these situations is not to make it worse while trying to make it *better*. If it's not health-related, sometimes we just need time to regroup and move forward. This could be walking away from it for a couple of hours, a day or more. We can live an optimistic lifestyle and philosophy with the goal to *Win the 16*, but we must know bad days are going to happen and execute strategies to deal with them.

Takeaways from this chapter include the following:

- Optimistic philosophy and lifestyles can coexist with negativity at times

- *Win the 16* was partially built on the concept that we live in a tough, complex and challenging world and at times, negativity seems to surround us

- Time to think by ourselves is important

- Self-reflection can help challenging situations

- *Win the 16* supports tough situations and bad days

- The world is amazing, but bad things or tough situations occur

- *Win the 16* can impact all our lives

Chapter 6 - Positivity

This chapter shares different ideas on positivity. Most people who know me well personally and professionally would describe me as a high-energy and positive person. Trust me, this section is not intended to convert or change people. It is written to share ideas that can be used by anyone with their employees, students, kids, and parents or themselves.

Positivity is not this over-the-top, "everything-is-perfect" mindset. It's a perspective to see the good in things. It is a mindset to work through the tough stuff knowing there is good on the other side. The optimistic thoughts that I carry often help me when things are not going well because they usually bring me back to thinking about things I am blessed with and thankful for. Gratitude is helpful in *Win the 16*. In my world, it's about choosing thoughts that can help me in most situations.

I tend to talk to myself. I believe in positive self-talk. I use it as a tool to motivate myself. It helps me fight through tough situations or moments. When things are not going well or when I want to stop, it is an optimal time for self-talk on positivity and optimism. Positive self-talk pushed me to overcome my self-inflicted barrier to write this book. I had talked about it many times but took no action. Have you ever sold yourself on why you can't do something? We all have. When we say we can't do something, it's more likely that we are choosing not to do that thing. Some reasons why we don't do things include:

- Don't have time
- Too busy
- Work
- Family
- Not changing our job in this economy or middle of the year
- Now is not the right time to do that because I have other stuff to do
- Next year
- I am tired
- Money

The positive self-talk supports me in many aspects of my life. I utilize it every day. For me to *Win the 16,* I must communicate positive things in my head to overcome the part of my brain that is telling me to stop. Our brains try to protect us. It can at times, allow negative thoughts to creep into our heads. If you are changing careers or leaving a job, your brain might fear that you can't do that, or you won't succeed. This is just more negative brain chatter. The chatter can stop us from achieving what we desire as well as inhibit us from going to the next level or making tough decisions. Unfortunately, noise in our heads can keep us from enjoyment and being happy. Have you allowed negative thoughts to impact being present in what should be a fun moment or experience? Yes. It happens to all of us.

One example could be Sunday night blues for those working early Monday morning. Many of us are already thinking about work instead of enjoying the moment. We need to be present with our friends, family, and most importantly ourselves. This is where positive self-talk can assist and adjust us mentally if we are cognizant of the "hijacking" in our brains.

In 2019, I committed to training for a triathlon, as did my sister-in-law, Joanne, and brother, Bud. They were wonderful, enthusiastic partners for me. Joanne had already completed this feat, so she was a professional to us. The athletic activities and distances that the Olympic triathlon consists of are the following:

- 0.93-mile swim
- 24.8-mile bike ride
- 6.2-mile run

To some, this journey might be relatively easy, and to others, it might seem impossible. I was optimistic, so I was in the middle. It was clearly a reachable goal, but it was not going to be easy. When I committed to doing this, it was November 2019, and the race was scheduled for July 2020.

I had just turned fifty years old, and since my goal is to live until I am one hundred, maybe this was my midlife crisis.

The training options were overwhelming. I finally found one that made the most sense and was approved by my fitness coach, Jack. I had one problem, a challenge if you will. I was not a strong swimmer. I would not drown in the water, but I had no idea how to breathe while swimming and knew nothing about proper, efficient swim strokes. I could throw my arms ahead of me to get from one end of the pool to another for a lap, but I certainly wasn't proficient enough to swim a mile.

My positive self-talk said, you can do this. It will be fine. One of my clients, Kent, was a good swimmer. We were discussing swimming, and he recommended a book called *Total Immersion* by Terry Laughlin with John Delves. I read the book in two weeks and had the plan mapped out for learning how to swim. I will set the scene for you. It is Chicago in December, cold and dark at 5:00 a.m. driving to the pool. At 5:15 a.m., with my book in hand plus videos on my phone, positive self-talk was what got me through that first week. I was frustrated and a bit embarrassed. I would swim one lap, look at the video or book, then do another. It was not easy, but with self-talk, I was progressing even though, I continued to struggle with breathing through my nose underwater, but I kept at it.

About a month into training, I was up to 400 meters, 16 laps, without stopping. I then befriended a guy at the gym, Kenny, who was in his mid-seventies. He became my unofficial swim coach. After a few weeks of Kenny's guidance, he became ill and was gone for a month. When he finally came back healthy, I thought I was swimming decently. Kenny didn't see it the same way. He yelled from the other end of the pool, "What are you doing?" I said, "I'm swimming." And he replied, "That's not swimming, that's drowning."

This was my welcome back from Kenny. He wasn't the most encouraging guy, but I so appreciated his ideas and teachings. He helped me. In the end, I learned how to swim, and it turned out swimming was not the hardest part of the triathlon. The last mile of the run was the worst part of the triathlon. We had a hot day. It was ninety-eight degrees. I did not mind the heat until the end of the run. It took three hours and twenty-four minutes to complete the triathlon. Many factors were involved, but the positive self-talk was imperative in learning how to swim, handling the frustrating days and ultimately completing my first triathlon. With just simple words, *you can do it. Don't stop! If others can, you can. It's only 10 or 20, or 30 more laps* that helped me tremendously.

I believe our mindset can drive us to amazing accomplishments or, alternatively, keep us from being our best selves if we let it. The brain is so powerful. I choose to use it to propel me to try to achieve great things. We have choices. We choose how we handle our own thoughts. We have agency.

For years, I had wanted to start my own consulting company, write a book, as well as create a podcast. When I did consulting work a few years back, I really enjoyed it. I worked with wonderful people, and our training was amazing. We helped our customers, and there was no question that it impacted organizations.

The dilemma in starting my own consulting business was I had a really good job at Alcon, working with quality people and some customers I'd known for years. I knew Alcon well since I was an employee for over twenty-years. I was blessed to be a part of an excellent, first-class organization.

I was driving to work at 6:30 a.m. for a meeting with the C-Suite of a large organization while listening to a podcast. They were discussing why people don't have the courage to take chances. The podcast listed some reasons people don't take risks: fear, lack of confidence, too comfortable, fixed mindset, laziness, etc. Fast forward a week. I was reading a book called, *Bet on You - How to Win with Risk* by Angie Morgan and Courtney Lynch. My interpretation of one of the messages in the book was that when people think about making a change or taking a chance, they think about the risk and what could go wrong. People fail to consider what the risk will be if they don't take the leap and make the change.

This reframed the risk for me. What I learned from both resources, my own vision, as well as my positive self-talk started to kick into high gear, I could do this. I started to believe I needed to do this. I had already done some research on the possibility of starting my own business, but I was inspired to do even more. Soon, it was crystal clear what I should do. This background work also prepared me for the naysayers, the ones who would say, "why would you do this? It's risky, etc.!" In my brain, I continued the positive self-talk and then made a call to my brother, my business guy, and a few others. Pygon ONE Consulting was formed. I am not saying that positive self-talk was the only reason I took the leap. But the positive self-talk helped me during the process. It helps me daily *Win the 16*.

One last thought on positivity. Positive energy helps us with discipline, creating habits and more. It brings early successes to the day and helps us overcome challenges. In leadership, we have people who crave and need positive energy. It is like food and water to them. It's imperative they get that. We know, though, at times, that is just not realistic. Negative things can happen, such as layoffs, bad performances, product recalls, and more. It's incumbent upon leaders to know which people need positive energy, so we can best support them during these times. There are also people on our teams and organizations who steal positive energy. The author Jon Gordon refers to people who steal energy as energy vampires in his fable, *The Energy Bus*. We all probably know family or friends who steal the energy out of a room.

I believe people that intentionally or unintentionally kidnap energy from our lives are a problem. If people in our lives take away our positive energy, it is harder for us to *Win the 16*. Those folks need to go. People who take energy from us and our environment can't be part of our quest. If you don't have the control to remove yourself from being around these individuals because they are a teammate or a coworker, it's critical you limit your exposure. Other people's views and negativity can be contagious. We can't allow them to sabotage our journey to being our best selves. Life is hard enough.

I conclude this chapter with a positive thought that sets an expectation on success, positive beliefs and outcomes and our mindset, which is the topic of the next chapter.

Desire to *Win the 16* daily because greatness awaits. We need to believe in ourselves, expect success, know that victory will occur, and wake up with a positive mindset to allow us the optimal opportunity to be our best selves.

Takeaways from this chapter include the following:

- Positivity and optimism are a choice

- Self-talk in a positive way can help overcome challenges

- Positive thoughts can help your mindset and perspective

- Beware of the people in your life who try to take away positive energy from you and the environment

- *Win the 16* can impact all our lives

Chapter 7 - Mindset

The last chapter on positivity leads perfectly into this chapter on mindset. How can you have the right mindset if you do not have the right attitude? We can control our mindset as well as our attitude. The type of mindset we have in different situations is a choice. It can always be altered. It's not easy, but it' a choice we all make. We have agency. In a work setting, when you have been asked to speak in front of the entire organization, it's natural to be nervous and excited. Is your mindset confident? Are you prepared? Are you visualizing how great your talk will be? Or is the focus on negative thoughts? Mindset is critical in this situation.

What if you must deliver bad news? Do you allow the situation to control your mindset? Do you rush to get it over with and lack empathy? Or do you deliver a calm, deliberate, empathetic and factual communication to the other person? Once again, mindset is critical.

There are two kinds of mindsets: fixed and growth. Most of us engage in both based on circumstances. Fixed mindsets are employed by people who don't have the conviction or belief that they can change their basic abilities, talents, skills and traits.

Growth mindsets are used by people who believe they can develop and advance through devotion to hard work. Writing this book is an excellent example of the growth mindset. I have never done this before and had no idea where to begin or how to write a book. The growth mindset was critical for me during this journey. This book has taught me so many things. It not only taught me about the process of being an author, but I also learned the business of writing a book. It challenged me to read even more. The research required when writing is extensive, and the journey has accelerated my growth and has raised my knowledge base to another level.

I am more advanced professionally, and a better leader and businessman because of this book. It would not have happened if I did not choose a growth mindset. In *Win the 16,* it's mandatory to implement some degree of growth mindset to continue to evolve and discover. Although there are times when having a fixed mindset is perfectly acceptable, it's always a good idea to be aware of growth possibilities.

In my past leadership roles, I have always articulated to my direct reports that when times get really challenging, you want me around. It's not arrogance, it's a belief system. I always performed better both academically and athletically when I stayed calm and didn't let the moment overtake me.

My kids and I enjoy the Batman movies, and just like the superhero, in stressful situations, it's critical to stay calm, think, exude confidence and act. Listening to understand is important in the process as well. Let me say that again. It's imperative during problems or bad times that we stay calm, actively listen and understand as much as possible. There is nothing worse than only knowing bits and pieces of the challenge or problem and then offering up ideas. It's critical to be authentic, so you must listen first to understand others. I like to fix things for people, so it's a watch out for me to let people share the entire story before I go into fix-it mode. This can be a challenge.

The mindset for me in tough situations is "it will work out". I just don't know how yet. Why? I have faith that, organically, things will work out. It might cause some work, pain and frustration along the way, but ultimately it will work out. If we can share this with people, it can be so helpful in the journey to *Win the 16*. Remember, we all need hope and confidence when we face challenges. Sometimes at work, you can feel there is no hope to manufacture enough products to meet demands, that the sales quota is not attainable, or the timeline to complete the academic curriculum is too tight. You might not meet the demand, but during the process, you could uncover an innovative way to improve production for the future that you never thought of, and this leads to other successes and achievements.

Yes, maybe quotas are unattainable, but you might outperform others by so much that the executives want you in the corporate home office for your exemplary effort. My point is that the possibilities are endless, and our mindset is imperative to helping or hurting our chances of future success. *Win the 16* preaches optimism and that we will get through this situation. It is a mindset that not only helps the situation, but is a more enjoyable way to live, adopt optimism and allow yourself the most optimal way to *Win the 16*.

A man named Jason *J-Mac* McElwain inspires me. He was diagnosed with autism at an early age and grew up facing and fighting the associated challenges. After reading his book, *The Game of my Life*, and watching his story on ESPN years ago, I learned how incredible he is. J-Mac demonstrates so many of the concepts in *Win the 16* I could use him as an example in most of the chapters.

J-Mac's life is a home run for the mindset chapter. He loved basketball, and he tried out for the high school basketball team, but he did not make the team. J-Mac wanted to be a part of the team somehow, so he became the team's manager for three years. It was his dream to play in a high school basketball game. In the last game of the year, J-Mac's dream became a reality when, with four minutes remaining, the coach put him in the game. The crowd went crazy. J-Mac took a shot and missed badly. Undeterred, he took another shot, but this time he made a three-pointer!

The crowd went wild, as you would expect. The game doesn't end on that made shot, however. J-Mac scored 20 points in those four minutes he was afforded. The night was epic and perfect. A lifelong dream was fulfilled by a young kid doing what he loves. When the horn went off, the students and players ran onto the floor, picked J-Mac up and carried him off. It was an amazing night for J-Mac, his family, and everyone who attended the game. They had no idea walking into that gym that Jason J-Mac McElwain was going to steal the show that night, as well as the hearts and minds of everyone in that building.

J-Mac embodies so many of the principles of *Win the 16*. His mindset is amazing, and he sets a strong example to never lose sight of your dream. After understanding his story, it's hard to put limits on myself. J-Mac had every reason to give up on his dream and have doubts. His thoughts didn't allow that. He pushed through, and that one-night, senior night on February 15th, 2006, his dream came true. Oh, the story has a twist, too. Every year, ESPN has an awards night for the best player, team, moment and more that they honor with an ESPY award. J-Mac was nominated that year for the best sports moment of the year, and his competition for the award included a sports team and two well-deserving players, one of whom was NBA professional basketball player Kobe Bryant.

For J-Mac to be nominated was incredible. Attending the award ceremony with such famous people was, I'm sure, an experience of a lifetime for a kid who just wouldn't quit or give up on his dream. This story can't get better, but it does. Yes, J-Mac won the ESPY award, and he stole the night on national TV. It's an amazing story and a wonderful example of unknowable possibilities and an incredible mindset.

This next example of mindset is a bit different than J-Mac's. It is an inspirational talk from Kara Lawson. She is the women's head basketball coach for Duke University. Coach

Lawson delivered a wonderful speech to her basketball team on making a mental shift and handling hard better. Some of Coach Lawson's accolades include:

- All-American at Tennessee University Women's basketball player
- Olympic Gold medal in basketball
- WNBA professional basketball player
- ESPN analyst
- Assistant coach Boston Celtics
- Head women's basketball coach at Duke University

1. Duke University Women's basketball website, October 31st, 2022.

Coach Lawson talked to her team about mindset. The highlights for me were her communication to handle hard better and how it's a mental shift and life doesn't get easier. Don't say to yourself, if I just get by this hard class or this hard moment, it will get easier, or just wait, and it will get easier. No, it won't get easier. You will need to handle hard better.

2. Kara Lawson, Handle Hard Better. YouTube video and transcript. July 5th,2022

This speech by Coach Lawson is incredible. Her message to her players to make a mental shift and change their mindset to handle hard better is a lesson for all of us. *Win the 16* is hard to accomplish, but it is achievable with small steps and commitment every day. Coach Lawson is 100 percent right. Life is hard! The great news is that we can not only make it, but we can also flourish. *Win the 16* principles can help us on the journey to succeed. *Win the 16* gives us a map to follow. In this chapter, we discussed how important mindset is as well as some incredible stories of how powerful it can be.

This chapter concludes by focusing on how companies communicate to their employees on what they value. Let's consider a hypothetical situation where we are seeking a position with an organization, and the following two items are important to that company.

1. Culture and a growth mindset are critical.

2. We trust our people. Our focus is results. No vacation policy, it's up to the employee to decide the days, weeks or months they take off.

Our mindset would most likely be positive if we were looking at a company with these values. Culture and a growth mindset is important to them, which means people are important to this organization. This is a wonderful thing. We would have a positive mindset about the company values. The second item on trust and allowing people to dictate when they go on vacation is incredibly empowering. The organization trusts its people and wants them to focus on producing positive results, not who works the most days. Performance is the measuring stick! I want to conclude this chapter with this because it's clear we can control our own mindset. People in charge of organizations, big or small, must know your values and trust in your people can drive a positive, optimistic mindset for your employees. Your decisions have an impact in so many ways. Companies can help their employees succeed when the right policies and values are communicated and demonstrated daily. Leading by example is always a good strategy.

Remember, leaders are not just the boss, executive team at work or physician at the hospital. All of us reading this have an opportunity to lead someone and to help support them. We can assist each other. All of us are leaders.

Takeaways from this chapter include the following:

- The type of mindset we have is a choice.

- Positive and optimistic mindsets can support and assist during tough times

- Never give up

- Dreams can come true, you just need to believe

- Life will not get easier

- Mental shift, handle the hard better

- Values and trust from employers impact workers' mindsets

- *Win the 16* can impact all our lives

Chapter 8 - Mental Toughness

Mental toughness can be viewed differently by all of us. Some might think of people who excel in physical activities such as professional football players, Navy SEALs, marathon runners, and stunt persons—all require mental toughness. Others might consider mental toughness to be intellectual aptitudes or emotional strength, such as what we might see in a professor, Bill Gates, a caregiver, or a single parent managing a tight family budget. Those people would be right, too. For some, mental toughness is situational. In certain environments, we could be mentally tough, but not in others. The good news is that mental toughness is a skill that can be improved.

In *Win the 16*, we believe mental toughness is important to optimizing your day. If you want to achieve a goal and better handle adversity, it absolutely takes mental toughness. Deep thought is pivotal to any goal-setting process. Also, it's important to truly think when adversity affects us. Quality time spent on what we want to achieve and how to handle challenges can take mental toughness. Time is a precious resource, so it can take mental determination to slow down to ensure proper time is spent on our goals and handling adversity.

Time by yourself without distractions builds mental toughness. It allows you to slow down and contemplate.

You have to say "no" at times to someone or something. It might mean sacrificing something that you enjoy or something you feel you need to do. Also, when you take time for yourself, be careful not to let your mind drift to thinking about responsibilities or obligations. Mental toughness is when you can put this all to the side and focus on the task at hand, which in this example is to just be alone to think. This is exhibiting mental toughness. You are emotionally making a sacrifice to be away from other things to just think. It can sound odd to some that we have to be mentally tough to just set time aside, but most of us need to do it.

Do our experiences in life affect how mentally tough we are? Yes. A kid who must wait for public transportation or walk to school eight blocks away in rain or snow on cold days must develop a certain amount of mental toughness. Can we improve our mental toughness? Yes. Mental toughness is a skill, and we can pursue growth in this area no matter where we are currently. In fact, if I don't work on my mental toughness, it will atrophy like an unused muscle. It is important we focus on it to maintain and grow our mental toughness.

As I reflect on my life, in the areas where success has occurred for longer periods of time, mental toughness has been demonstrated. A lawyer or physician that routinely spent hours by themselves at the library, passed all those classes, and board exams, sleep deprivation at times, and sacrificed social engagements and sections of their life to ensure they meet their goal of becoming a lawyer and doctor is exuding mental toughness. This does not happen overnight. The success materialized due to sustained mental toughness over time. All of us have demonstrated mental toughness in some capacity in our lives. In *Win the 16*, it's imperative that mental toughness is part of the daily journey. It's critical that we believe in ourselves to be mentally tough and work at it because we can develop it. In previous chapters, we discussed mindset, positivity and motivation. Have you ever needed to be positive or optimistic for someone in a painful or challenging moment? If so, that takes mental toughness.

I could not write a book, let alone a chapter on mental toughness, without mentioning a man who is incredibly mentally tough. His name is David Goggins. He was an out-of-shape young man growing up without much focus, discipline or mental toughness who decided to turn his life around. Here are some of his accomplishments:

- Navy SEAL
- Army Ranger school
- Air Force Tactical air controller training
- Sixty ultra-marathons

How does an out-of-shape undisciplined young man do all of this? There are many traits and attributes Goggins developed, including mental toughness. He is an expert at overcoming the chatter in his brain that tells him to stop doing something or to give up. His ability to self-talk to eliminate negative chatter and do what he has set out to do is an inspiration. He has found an avenue to master his mind and thoughts to overcome so many physical and mental challenges. When he speaks, his addiction to hard work is crystal-clear. Clearly, David Goggins has the mental toughness and has brought himself to a juncture where he can go above and beyond what our minds want us to do.

His accomplishments and his mindset shows us that we do have the ability to dig a bit deeper than we think we can. I shared earlier in the book the power of positive self-talk. By improving and increasing our mental toughness and positive self-talk, it can help us attack a challenge or overcome a tough situation and enable us to keep marching on towards our goals. Some small challenges could be to read for fifteen minutes a day, get up fifteen minutes earlier than usual or go to bed fifteen minutes earlier than normal. If David Goggins can do what he does, can we give more? Where can we uncover opportunities to increase our mental toughness? When we must make a courageous decision, can we do it? Yes, we can. Again, it's a choice.

Here is a tough hypothetical for executives, leaders or directors. Sales are lower than expected for the launch of a new product. Pressure is coming from above to increase sales and take action. Do you force change and action just because of the pressure? You know the marketing and sales teams are doing the right things, but the heat is coming from above. Do you have the mental toughness to say you will turn this around, but we are staying the course because I believe in the plan? This takes a tremendous amount of grit, courage and mental toughness.

In *Win the 16* to optimize your day and be your best self, it's going to take not only hard work, but mental toughness whether you are faced with a physical challenge or an intellectual challenge. No one principle in this book is more important than the others. They all play off each other. If we can think of David Goggins tomorrow when we are going through a challenge, it could propel us to do something we normally wouldn't do. When we squash the chatter persuading us not to do something hard, we become mentally tough. One day at a time.

During our journey in mental toughness, we need to remember most of us want to be in a place that is happy and safe. Also, we are probably willing to work and handle some suffering and pain in terms of mental toughness, but only to a degree. If we exceed our limit of pain or discomfort, what would the possibilities be? We don't know until we do it. It's not easy. The key to improving this mental toughness skill is to go past that point where you want to stop or quit. Go beyond! It's hard, but we can do it.

Here are a couple of tips for you:

- Deep breaths to relax, reduce stress and brain chatter

- Positive self-talk, you can do it

- Visually think about the end and how accomplished as well as proud you could feel when you get to the end

- Small steps in your growth are amazing, don't try to overdo it

Mental toughness is a skill. It can be developed. There are many programs and challenges to improve it. It is incumbent upon you to decide whether this is a skill you want to improve. Choosing a small challenge, task, or program could assist your growth. I completed the 75 HARD challenge twice. It has mental and physical components to complete for 75 consecutive days. It was challenging and rewarding.

In November 2022, I decided to create my own mental and physical challenge that consisted of things that aren't natural or enjoyable to me. The mental challenge consisted of meditating and breathing exercises, physical activity in the cold weather, and journaling every day for thirty-eight straight days. Personally, I enjoy variety in life and my workouts.

This challenge was going to test my mindset due to boredom. Here was my thirty-eight straight day challenge starting December 9th, 2022:

1. Three minutes of meditation and breathing exercises

2. Completing an outdoor MURPH workout

3. Journaling post-workout

The MURPH is a popular CrossFit workout named after a fallen Navy SEAL, Lieutenant Michael Murphy. In honor of him, it is typically performed on Memorial Day. It consists of the following:

- One-mile run
- 100 pull-ups
- 200 push-ups
- 300 air squats
- Another one-mile run

*All done wearing a twenty-pound vest, if you can.

The morning arrived on December 9th, and the challenge began. I struggle with meditation and breathing exercises, so I committed to focusing deeply. The MURPH workout is one I enjoy, and I usually complete it in 37 to 40 minutes with the vest. The challenge with the MURPH was going to be the monotony of doing the same workout every day, wearing the vest and in cold temperatures. Finally, I had not journaled routinely since a friend, Casey Richardson, and I committed to it years ago for twenty-one straight days.

On the first day, I completed all my tasks. The weather was good at 31 degrees. I was laser-focused, and felt good. Fast-forward to day 16, Christmas Eve. For three consecutive days, the weather was between negative 20 and 40 degrees with the wind. The phone rings, and it's my brother, Dr. Pygon. He said you can't do the challenge outside. It's too cold. We compromised, so I did the running outside and the other exercises inside. He was right, always better to be safe than sorry.

January 15th was the last day of the challenge, and I was thrilled to complete it for many reasons. I improved my ability to meditate and breathe more effectively. It's still a focus issue, but I am better. The MURPH challenged my mindset due to the boredom and the cold at times. Also, I had to manage my left knee with ice to control the inflammation. In *Win the 16*, earlier, we discussed unforeseen challenges. My knee became my challenge. I changed course at the end.

For the last eight days, I didn't wear the 20-pound vest to give my knee additional relief, and it worked. The journaling continued to be tough because whenever time wasn't on my side, I wanted to not journal. I literally had to force myself to do it. In the end, I was glad I did it. The reflections of the day, challenges, learnings, plans, failures, goals, accomplishments, and results were good to read. Did this mental challenge push me into uncomfortable territory and improve my mental toughness? Yes.

Please understand, it doesn't matter what type of challenge you do. It is the process you are developing for future challenges and adversity in your life. You are creating a pathway for success when you need it, no matter what the obstacle will be. Pick anything that is a bit of a struggle for you and complete it daily for a certain period. It could be not eating after 6 pm, no sugar, journaling, or jogging daily for 15 minutes, no matter the weather. The great thing about this is that it's yours. I am not recommending my challenge to anyone. I can't do what David Goggins does. He does what is good for him. You need to find what is best for you. Just remember, mental toughness is a skill. We can work to improve it. Also, remember that if you select a physical challenge, you should notify your healthcare provider prior to starting to ensure safety.

In concluding this chapter, I encourage you to find an aspect of mental toughness that you would like to improve and then identify or create a challenge for yourself that you must overcome or accomplish. We have the power to progress and improve mental toughness. The feeling of accomplishment when we progress and fight through tough moments is something special. We need to celebrate these wins no matter how small or big they are. Life is meant to enjoy our successes.

Takeaways from this chapter include the following:

- Mental Toughness is a skill, so you can learn and develop it

- Mental Toughness can help us with intellectual and physical challenges

- We want to be in a happy place and safe environment, but we can go farther and deeper

- Mental strength challenges can increase our mental toughness

- Overcoming tough mental and physical challenges can be rewarding

- Create your own mental toughness challenge

- *Win the 16* can impact all our lives

Chapter 9 -
Early Success in your Day

Some people are morning people. Some are not. This chapter is not intended to change your sleeping habits. You can decide what is best for you. The concept of early successes in our day is to challenge us to explode out of bed into our day feeling good. In the definition of *Win the 16,* it states, "Early successes in your day can cascade into more successes throughout your day. Whatever time you start your day, *Win the 16* can support your waking sixteen hours." No matter the time, you rise every minute and every hour in the day can demand more of you. Our days can move quickly, and before you know it, we spend most of the day on other people's agendas and priorities. This is one of the reasons early successes in our days are critical. Personally, I want to *Win the 16* by 10 a.m.

The question is, how do we have early successes that will propel us to even more success? This chapter shares ideas and strategies for successes we can achieve early in the day. Hopefully, it helps you to uncover more ideas of potential early successes in your day.

Some people just try to equip themselves to wake up and survive the crazy, busy morning, whether it's getting themselves going and off to work or the parents who get kids off to school. The mornings can be quite busy, so how can I get an early success? First, we need to define what an early success is in your day. An early success is when you engage in and complete an act that makes you feel proud and accomplished. It's an act that requires discipline, contributes to something you value and is done in a timely manner. You decide the time this act takes.

A positive mindset is step one in starting your day. If you are a person who does not jump out of bed, I understand. But to start the day with energy is a decision we can make. Is it fair to wake up and focus on having a good start to your day? Yes. Being enthusiastic about the potential of that day could be a success for you if that is not your typical morning mindset. Whatever you can do to start your day right has to fit your personality and style. The morning ritual for Susan, my wife, and I is saying, good morning, and I love you. This works for us and helps us start our day.

The first thing military women and men do upon waking up is make their bed. This is something that Susan and I have adopted, as well. By no means am I comparing us to our brave military. What I am communicating is that we can emulate the discipline and task accomplishment example the military sets. US Navy Admiral William H. McRaven, commander of the forces who organized the raid to assassinate Osama bin Laden, once delivered a commencement speech at the University of Texas that has since become famous. One takeaway from the speech for me was that if you want to change the world, start off by making your bed.

In other words, small accomplishments early in the day can lead to bigger things. This is exactly what early successes are to *Win the 16*. Create a habit and start your days with a win, no matter the size. Small wins early in our day not only support our mindset, but they can also propel us to even more success the rest of the day.

Here are some ideas for early successes in the morning.

- **Take a walk.** Take a walk outside, no matter the weather to jump-start your day. Even ten minutes in the great outdoors is a nice start to your day. If you do that every day, it is a nice accomplishment and an act of discipline to start your day. You can be proud of that. Just remember, it must be a consistent routine.

- **Rehydrate.** Another idea is to drink a glass of water immediately upon waking up. The data supports that a great many of us are dehydrated, especially first thing in the morning. Some people have a glass by their bed ready to fill up and drink first thing.

- **Read.** Read for ten minutes for your own personal development or inspiration. This is about you. The book could be about development for your personal or professional life.

- **Practice meditation.** Meditation is a practice that is incredible for breathing, relaxing, focusing the mind and more.

- **Express gratitude.** Either say out loud or write in a journal what you are thankful for each morning.

- **Exercise.** Exercise at whatever pace is recommended by your healthcare professional. The feeling you get after a workout could completely jump-start your day and propel you into a wonderful morning. It helps you inside and out. Personally, I love my morning workouts. It boosts my energy, improves focus and cognition, patience, better mood, improves the quality of sleep, and supports a healthy eating routine.

- **Don't check your e-mail right away.** For those who jump on email early in the morning or first thing at work, consider not checking email until you accomplish a task, priority or something for yourself. It is empowering to control the beginning of your day with your priorities, and the things you need to do to *Win the 16*. Email messages routinely put you on the defensive, spending time on what is important to others instead of being on the offensive, meaning spending time on your agenda. Time is our most valuable resource. It's our responsibility to ensure we are managing our morning properly. To be our best selves, we need to win our mornings or whenever our day begins.

- **Send a positive message to someone.** Share with someone how much you appreciate them or send any message that would jump-start their day.

No matter what we decide to do or stop doing, early successes in your day can make us feel good about ourselves as well as launch us into our day with the right mindset and a win. You just need to figure out what is best for you. In the prior chapters, we discussed mindset and mental toughness at length and how it affects our *Win the 16*. The first thing in the morning, before we engage with the outside world, we have a choice on the mindset and mental toughness we bring as we begin the day.

Win the 16 is much more enjoyable, and it's easier to accomplish what we want that day if we wake up with an optimistic mindset, complete a task early on, do something positive for ourselves or others, or share gratitude that supports our journey that day. I didn't say this was easy, but these successes don't have to be major. The habits you are developing will not just help your mindset but will also help you with the next challenge or success that could be larger. The process is the same, no matter the size of the challenge. You need the right mindset, mental toughness, positive self-talk, habits, discipline and more. You are building a process and path.

Takeaways from this chapter include the following:

- Early successes in our days can lead to more success in our sixteen waking hours

- Rising in the morning is a privilege with a lot to be thankful for

- Small tasks completed, such as making our bed or drinking water or ten-minute walks, are doable successes to start your day

- Tell someone else early in the morning how you appreciate and respect them. Makes you and them feel good

- *Win the 16* can impact all our lives

Chapter 10 - Goals

All of us have different perspectives on goal setting. I believe in goals. I write them down and keep them in front of me to ensure I stay focused on them. Writing them down also helps me because I am a visual learner. My brain is wired in a way that if I can see it, I can achieve it. The visualization of a goal is imperative for accomplishing the goal. *Win the 16* has many principles and strategies to it, and having your goals visible will support you in reaching those goals. When I think of goal-oriented people, a few jump right out for me. Bill Gates, Michael Jordan, Oprah Winfrey, David Goggins and Jason McElwain (J-Mac from earlier in the book). They have many attributes, values and skills that drive them to massive success. Each had goals, and they were driven to achieve them. In fact, they wanted to conquer their goals.

Some people say goals just die once you accomplish that specific goal. They believe that once you achieve them, that goal is over. I look at it differently in *Win the 16,* and I believe that once you hit a goal, you should celebrate and enjoy the moment. As a leader, I believe in celebrating victories no matter the size. If people hit a goal, no matter how large or small, that is a cause for celebration. It is a missed opportunity for leaders, teams and people when they do not celebrate victories. Not only is it motivating for people to be recognized and valued, but it also supports a strong culture and demonstrates appreciation for the work and effort being done.

Also, individuals need to celebrate and reflect on the achievements. We get adrenaline from being successful and meeting a goal or objective. It must be recognized. If anyone reading this book never works out in the morning or walks in the morning before work, but you do that for the next five days because you set that goal, you need to celebrate that goal on day 5. I am proud of you, and you should be, too. We can make another goal to challenge for additional success or even greater achievements later, but right now, in the moment, celebrate. It's healthy, inspiring and leads to more success. You are winning the sixteen. It's one day at a time, one step forward. We need to praise these small wins.

Are goals important? Do we need to set goals? In *Win the 16*, we are 100 percent behind setting goals. They need to be genuine, authentic and well-thought-out. Deep thought is a must when setting goals. *Win the 16* is a contemplative program. The individual implementation needs to be well-designed. It's critical to take time, dig deep, and think about your goals. We have discussed motivators, inspiration, positivity, mindset, mental toughness, and early successes in your day, which could cascade into more successes. Each of these is relevant to the goals.

Motivation and inspiration are the drivers of our goals. They play a role in what our goals are and how we devise them. We must be inspired to hit our objectives. Mental strength and a positive mindset are also important. The goals we set are meant to be challenging while pushing us to greater success. It is critical to be positive, and tough-minded to stay on our expedition and work through the tough moments, which will come with any goal that pushes us. Stretch goals can position our growth and success even more when it is time to set that objective above and beyond. We have moments in life to reflect upon in which we completed a feat far beyond what we ever thought. Remembering those moments should be motivation for future success.

I was 100 percent stretched writing this book and starting a podcast while also leading my company. The small goals set forth during this expedition were helpful. Small goal setting keeps us on pace to meet the larger goal at the end. I can't stress it enough, if you have a lengthy goal, you need to have smaller goals to attain on your quest for the larger goal. It gives you something to aim for that is reachable sooner rather than later. It helps us move forward. We will discuss in the next couple of chapters habits and discipline, skills that help us achieve our goals. Below, I am going to share different objectives that were achieved, and some of them, to say the least, were stretch goals of historical significance. These serve as examples of the importance of goal setting.

In May of 1961, John F. Kennedy declared in an unforgettable speech that the United States of America should commit itself to achieve the goal, before the decade was out, of landing a man on the Moon and returning him safely to the Earth.

Wow! I remember this from history class. What a goal President Kennedy put forth for not only the United States, but the entire world. At the time, Russia was ahead of the United States in the space race. Many people did not believe there was any chance this could happen. Well, it did happen. The United States met President Kennedy's goal. On July 20, 1969, the United States of America made history when our astronauts took their first steps on the moon.

Just over forty years ago, Bill Gates, co-founder of Microsoft, said that every desk will have a computer. The statement is universally known. But, if we could walk back in time, that was a bold statement and goal. There were doubters that this would happen. Bill Gates and his partner Paul Allen were committed to seeing their vision become a reality. They articulated a stretch goal and delivered.

The Cold War was the geopolitical, ideological and economic struggle between two world superpowers, the USA and the Union of Soviet Socialist Republics (USSR). In the 1970s and 1980s, to use the term 'rivalry' to describe the relationship between the United States and USSR would be kind.

The Winter Olympics were in the United States at Lake Placid, New York, in 1980. I remember those Olympic Games like it was yesterday. Everyone who was alive in that era would probably remember the 1980 Winter Olympics. The scenario in Lake Placid was picturesque for the winter games. It was snowy and beautiful. There was one sport and one team that stole the show at these games, and they are now historic in the sports world. I still recall the "miracle on ice", which is how people characterize what was accomplished.

Prior to 1980, Herb Brooks was selected to coach the 1980 USA Olympic hockey team. This is an incredible honor and an opportunity to win a gold medal in hockey at the Winter Olympics, something the USA hasn't done in twenty years. It was also nearly impossible. The winter hockey Olympics were dominated by the USSR hockey team since their players were professional players. The USA hockey team consisted of amateur players because, at that time professional players were not allowed to participate per USA rules.

Coach Brooks set a goal for his young players to be the best team in the world and win the Olympics. To do that, they would have to beat USSR, which prior to the Winter Olympics, the USA hockey team lost to them 10-3. It was professionals playing amateurs, and the gap in experience and accomplishments was tremendous. USSR was the best hockey team headed into the Olympics.

It is now February 22nd, 1980, and the USA Winter Olympics hockey team is playing the incredibly talented, experienced, and heavily favored USSR to see who will play in the gold medal game. It was an accomplishment already that the USA team was even in this game. I was at Chicago Mt. Carmel High School that day, watching my oldest brother's basketball game.

The night turned into an epic evening because the USA hockey team beat the USSR in one of the greatest upsets in the sport's history. As the game was coming to an end Al Michaels, the TV sports announcer for that game, delivered a historic call. He said, "do you believe in miracles?" It was clearly a David vs. Goliath story, plus it happened in Lake Placid, New York, with all the political backdrop issues going on between the two superpowers. The USA hockey team went on and two days later won the gold medal. I still get goosebumps thinking about the "USA" chants during those games.

In this chapter, I shared three unthinkable goals that were achieved. *Win the 16* is not designed to tell you how aspirational your goals should be. Rather, it is to share that few things are possible unless you set a goal and have a vision. Things don't happen by chance. *Win the 16* believes in thoughtful goal setting and agency, controlling your destiny and goals play a role. Go attain what you desire! Normal, everyday people achieve greatness all the time. Why not you? Remember, your goals don't have to be large, extraordinary reaches. Small steps and small goals can lead to winning the sixteen.

Takeaways from this chapter include the following:

- Goals are helpful to *Win the 16*

- They must be authentic and well thought-out

- We need to dig deep with a positive mindset to uncover our optimal goals

- Most great things happen with a goal in mind

- Amazing things will not be achieved without stretch goals, like President Kennedy, Bill Gates, and Herb Brooks demonstrated

- Goals can be small ones, built one step at a time

- *Win the 16* can impact all our lives

Chapter 11 - Habits

Win the 16 believes habits are instrumental to optimizing your day. If you are motivated to go for a walk, is it likely you will do that? Yes, because your mindset is in that place where you want to go and do something. At work, if you want a promotion, you will do all you can to put yourself in the best position to be a viable candidate. You know how competitive it is to earn this position. Sometimes you stay late after work. Sometimes you do not. You hear that every night this week, the executive team is meeting after regular hours. Are you more willing to stay late this week? Yes. Why? Because you are motivated to get the promotion and the executives will be there. What happens when we aren't motivated, and we don't want to go for a walk after dinner even though we know it's good for us? We might make excuses or justifications for not doing it, and the bottom line is that we don't go for a walk. This is a simple example, but it shows why motivation is powerful and what happens when it's absent.

Are we motivated twenty-four hours a day, seven days a week? No. None of us are motivated to do things all the time. If we create habits, however, they will take over and get us through when we aren't motivated. Habits enable us to do the hard stuff even when we don't want to. No one can *Win the 16* without building quality habits. Small changes can lead to major results in the end. This principle is imperative to the success of *Win the 16*. If a person has good habits with laser-focus to achieve a goal, and a sprinkle of discipline, there is a higher probability that they will meet or exceed their goal.

Most people would agree habits are not a novel idea. I can remember the old food pyramid in grade school that was intended to help create quality food habits. We know there are wonderful habits and not-so-wonderful habits that we do. Before I share potential good habits that assist you in winning your sixteen, let's examine what holds us back from creating more high-quality habits and stops us from eliminating some bad habits. Here is one at the top of the list: time. Many of us would like to do certain things, but a perceived lack of time holds us back. Someone might like to read every day, but they don't believe they have the time due to the many other obligations that have to be done.

How about a bad habit due to time? Texting while driving is an example of a bad habit. People do it for many reasons, but for some, it could be time because they think they need to communicate immediately, or they worry they won't have time later. Our food choices can also be related to time. I might believe that I don't have time to go to the store, so I decide to eat fast food. If we create a good habit for situations like these, with a dash of discipline, it's amazing how much we can accomplish along with eliminating bad habits.

Lack of change agility or complacency may also prevent some from creating new, healthy habits. Change agility is the desire to accept change and a sense of adaptability. In our world, it's constant. To *Win the 16,* you must embrace it as a positive potential opportunity, not fear it. It might not be natural for you to change and interrupt your comfortable routine, but it's critical to be your best self. Some people stay in jobs and professions because they are complacent. Their role no longer fulfills or motivates them to learn and grow to explore their potential. They just do the identical work each day. They may be afraid of change, unwilling to put the work into discovering the possibilities or lack change agility. Individuals who struggle with change agility need to make small habit changes, so they don't get overwhelmed. This allows them to absorb the feeling of the good new habit while deleting the old habit.

Another reason could be mindset and mental toughness, as discussed earlier in the book. The mind tries to protect us. If our actions are based on habit, our brains feel comfortable and protected. It's hard to change that habit. My brother, Dr. Bud Pygon, is an anesthesiologist at the University of Illinois at Chicago. He was always an athlete and healthy. He let himself go a little bit, and he was not meeting his self-imposed physical standard. He told his trainer that he wanted more. His trainer told him that he had to work out regularly, but Bud thought he didn't have time. His trainer asked him to get up thirty minutes earlier a few times a week for two weeks. This meant Bud had to wake up even earlier, and like most doctors they are already rising early in the morning.

It forced Bud to be disciplined to go to bed earlier, so he was rested in the morning. Getting up in the dark in the winter was painful. It absolutely took mental toughness and mindset to try this new habit and continue with it. Many years later, waking early to exercise has become a permanent habit for him. Bud is fifty-nine years old now. I share this because no matter our ages, we can change our habits. It can be challenging, but it's possible. Changing habits takes discipline and mental toughness to happen successfully. We have a choice to adjust our current habits and create new ones.

If a task is difficult, your ability to be strong mentally is imperative to achieve what you desire. Overcoming time, lack of change agility, and lacking the right mindset are real. Our mental toughness can help propel us through. Habits can sustain us during times where we lack motivation, inspiration and when life can become stressful and overwhelming. Our habits just become what we do no matter what role our situation or emotions play. Inevitably habits will define our ability to optimize our day.

If we have good habits, they will take us through whatever emotion or challenge that is stopping us. Habits are built by our desire to change, to learn, and to set goals. They are based on our discipline, creating a routine and training. The more we are equipped and trained to handle situations, the better the outcome. Habits play a role in our success.

Small habits can lead to amazing results. This chapter concludes with an interesting example of the power of habits. This person exhibits habits as well as many of the principles in *Win the 16*.

Earlier, I shared an accomplishment that I am very proud of, which was learning how to swim effectively at fifty years old and completing two Olympic triathlons. Remember that it is a 0.93-mile swim, 24.8-mile bike ride and 6.2-mile run. My inspirations for doing this were many. My friend Casey Richardson is an Ironman. He taught me how mentally and physically challenging an Ironman race is for all participants. He also taught me the importance of attention to detail and preparation regarding training, nutrition, rest, time-management, course correcting, equipment involved, and more. I have so much respect for women and men that train and compete in the Ironman race.

One person that should be an inspiration to all is Chris Nikic. I have shared his story with many in conversation. I remember watching the highlights of him on TV and the internet. Just fell in love with the story. He is the first person with Down Syndrome to complete an Ironman, which is a 2.4-mile swim, 112-mile bike ride and a 26.2-mile run. He finished the race in sixteen hours and forty-six minutes and nine seconds. He beat the seventeen-hour clock. How did this young man do it? His book title says it all, *1 Percent Better: Reaching my Full Potential and How You Can Too*. Chris' mindset was about getting a little better each day.

This isn't a new concept. The difference is that Chris believed in the concept and lived it. He just got a little better every day. The discipline to focus on getting 1 percent better every day is impressive. Many would struggle with that because the results might not be fast enough. We want to get to where we want to go quicker. It's not easy, but if we can stay focused on small steps and small wins, it will help achieve major results over time. This can help us incrementally move forward daily and never stop. Chris never stopped getting 1 percent better. The habits he demonstrated were impressive.

Chris has more challenges than most to overcome. He doesn't allow those challenges to inhibit his ability to be successful. He defines his own success and doesn't let obstacles become insurmountable. One of the reasons I shared this story is because Chris can inspire us on days we aren't at our best and need some help. His habits and commitment to progress can assist us on our journey to *Win the 16*.

Takeaways from this chapter include the following:

- Habits are pivotal to winning the sixteen

- Habits and discipline are what we lean on when motivation is not available

- Time and mindset can sabotage our true desires. Don't let them

- A little better every day can lead to results over time

- *Win the 16* can impact all our lives

Chapter 12 - Discipline

Hearing the word discipline could evoke images of disciplining our kids or being disciplined. We might think of our military for all their disciplined behavior. Maybe now David Goggins or Chris Nikic come to mind when we hear the word discipline. *Win the 16* defines discipline as our ability to act regardless of the situation or how we feel emotionally or physically. Discipline for myself is when I look in the mirror, and every ounce of my mind and body says, I do not want to do this right now, but my discipline kicks in, and I will do it. To me, this is so pivotal in *Win the 16* because motivation at times will not be there, so this is when habits and discipline take over and ensure we do what is necessary to accomplish our goals.

Some people confuse willpower and discipline. I view willpower as the ability to walk by the dessert table and not have a piece of the pie. Discipline is the self-control to do it all the time. It's in your mindset that you won't even think about giving in to dessert. You demonstrate disciplined behaviors that are just always on. You just live a certain way. Self-discipline is resisting temptations, so you can stay on your path in the direction you are heading. It's not easy. The good news it is a skill, so it can be developed and focused on.

My morning routine involves saying a couple of gratitudes and telling my wife, Susan, that I love her, whether I am at home or traveling for business. We make the bed. It's what we do. I share this because the little things in life can be the hardest. It takes discipline and focus to execute. This leads me to my next morning ritual, which is a cold shower for no less than two minutes. It wakes me up. It's invigorating. I feel great afterwards. The next discipline is to perform thirty push-ups no matter what. My mindset is now ready to attack the day.

On one of our *Win the 16* podcasts, we shared a challenge of walking first thing in the morning, outside preferably, for ten to thirty minutes every day for thirty-one days. The timing of the challenge was November 15th to December 15th, so the weather could be cold and snowy. I started doing that routinely in conjunction with my morning workouts. This meant I had to get up earlier to fit that in, which meant I had to change my nightly schedule to go to bed earlier. The walk outside with water or coffee in the fresh air and light if the sun is up creates a phenomenal way to start your day. Unfortunately, many mornings in Chicago, it's still dark, but it's refreshing to start your day outside in the fresh air. These disciplines are not for everyone. My hope is that you will read these ideas and then implement what makes sense for you. This is your canvas to create whatever fits your lifestyle, goals, and desires and stretches you a bit. In the book, we discussed early successes in the day. One of these routines could be your early success in your day. Also, you might create your own activity that makes sense for you, which is fantastic. Discipline is crucial to *Win the 16*.

Small steps and small changes lead to great results. To *Win the 16,* we all need the discipline to optimize our days. These small actions can really help to start our day off the right way. Another discipline for some is going to work and completing a task before they check their e-mail. For some, that would take tremendous discipline. Just pick one positive change for tomorrow and make it small, so you can start with a success.

The father-son love story below is about many things, including discipline and the principles in *Win the 16*. You might have heard of Team Hoyt. They are universally known. I was first introduced to them by ESPN. They have been discussed on news channels, written about in numerous articles, and a book has been published about their story. Rick Hoyt is an incredible man who was born with cerebral palsy. He doesn't have the gift of being able to run. His late father, Dick, decided to do something unthinkable for Rick and compete in numerous Ironman races, triathlons, and marathons. One catch, Rick joined him on these races. How is that possible if Rick has these limitations?

First, I am not sure the Hoyt team ever saw limitations in life. Just a guess! To participate in the races together, Dick pushed Rick in a special chair for the running section, swam, pulling him in a small float for the swimming part, and towed him in a special seat for the bike portion. This story is something special. It's a love story first. Using only the term 'discipline' to describe what the Hoyts did does not do them justice because they embody all the principles in *Win the 16*. The Hoyt team is an inspiration to all on countless levels.

Let's conclude this chapter with how discipline can help us and how to build it. Discipline is a pillar in *Win the 16* because we can't be our best selves without it.

Discipline assists us in the following ways:

- Organized – Create the time to be systematic

- Proficiency at work – Focus on priorities and completing major projects can be the result

- Increase mind and body health – Do the right things to help yourself

- Persistence and resiliency – Stay focused on the task and bounce back from adversity

- Lacking motivation and inspiration – Discipline and habits can push us through

Ideas to build discipline:

- Surround yourself with disciplined people

- Small tasks completed every day

- Write down your goals, write them on a sticky note and place it on your bathroom mirror

- Visualize daily what you want

- Start small

- Accountability partner, coach or mentor to keep you focused and progressing

- Measure progress

- Identify struggle areas and strengths

- Start immediately, don't wait to begin

- Mindset means you control your discipline, nobody else

- Remove yourself from people, places, and situations that challenge your quest to develop your discipline

- Admit it's not easy, but you can be more disciplined

Takeaways from this chapter include the following:

- Discipline is what supports and helps us achieve things when we are not motivated

- Willpower and discipline are not the same things

- We can create habits and acts of discipline

- Discipline can help us do amazing things

- We control our discipline, no one else

- Discipline is a skill, so it can be developed

- *Win the 16* can impact all our lives.

Chapter 13 – Time Management

Time is beautiful! It is a gift as well as a blessing that we are awarded each day, no matter what happened the day before. Yes, some days and weeks can be long and arduous, but for most of us, time goes by so fast. People often wish they had more time in a day to get more work done, read, workout or spend with someone they love. I share these moments and start this chapter in this manner because most of us desire to accrue more time in our days, or we wish we had more time. In this chapter, we are going to dive into time management with potential ways to help you propel your days, so you can *Win the 16*.

This will take some self-examination of your daily activities. Before we jump in, I request you to read this chapter from the perspective that time is beautiful and precious. I want you to think of time as invaluable because it will assist you in finding more of it, as well as managing it more effectively. Many go to bed wondering where the day went. We need to investigate uncovering additional time in our twenty-four-hour day to put toward areas that we deem important, and the answer is not to compromise sleep, which is crucial to our health.

There are situations when the real, influential and important people in your life need your time. Customers call about a challenge. Your kids still need dinner even though you're on deadline at work. Our employees need to feel as valued as our bosses. Too many times, we create time for the boss at the expense of our trusted employees. A mistake I made in the past was excusing myself from a conversation on the phone with a direct report because my boss or leader was calling. It was done politely, but it's still not right. I had one colleague in leadership who, if he was in the field with an employee all day, wouldn't take any calls or texts. I share that not to recommend that, but his commitment to being present while with his direct report was impressive.

One way we can find additional time in our day is by identifying time thieves, which are people or events in our professional and personal lives who steal our time. Unfortunately, we can't always control who takes up our time. The question is, how many people do we have in our lives who are extracting too much of our precious time in situations that are not critical or a priority, and are potentially infringing our ability to *Win the 16*? These people must be identified, and our interaction with them must change. It could be uncomfortable at first, but it's imperative to *win the 16* that you take back some time in your days. We must change our mindset and behaviors when these people are about to snatch our valuable minutes.

Let's discuss a few other examples of time thieves.

- Calls or texts that aren't critical personally or professionally
- E-mail and more e-mail
- Social media distractions such as Twitter, Instagram, TikTok, Facebook, YouTube and more

- No specific plan, or even a partial plan, on the day's priorities
- Allowing mismanaged meetings to stretch beyond the time you allotted
- Not keeping your own meetings to the time allocated
- Non-urgent business matters that could wait
- Overscheduling your sixteen-hour days
- Not being able to say "no" to people
- Trying to fix everyone's problems at work or at home
- Work that could and should be delegated
- Micromanagement at home and work
- TV
- Gossip articles and conversations
- Performing someone else's job or responsibilities
- Not asking for help on a project or problem at work and home

Time is precious and invaluable. It's pivotal we treat it that way. Now let's share some ideas that we can use to help support our time management challenges.

Step 1 – Recognize we have time management issues. If you have ever said, "I would like to do that, but I don't have time," then you have a time management issue. Please don't take that as a negative. The point is you want to do something in your sixteen-hour day, but you don't because you perceive a lack of time. This is a problem and shouldn't be neglected. We can all benefit from better time management, especially if there's something we want to do and currently don't have time for. If you have something you would like to add to your organization, department or for yourself, time management is important and something most of us struggle with.

Step 2 - Reframe a time management problem into a time management opportunity. This is a good thing. It's a positive way to look at this. We have an opportunity in front of us.

Step 3 - PLAN your day, the day before. In *Win the 16,* you have sixteen hours to work with. Schedule that day to ensure your goals and priorities are being attended to the first thing. If you want to get a thirty-minute workout completed twice a week, it's imperative that you work it into your schedule. If you want to set time aside for your own development, plan it in your schedule. Make sure it's on your calendar.

Step 4 - Critical items go first! Prioritize each day's critical items first thing. Schedule items that are not imperative after that. Accomplish the critical things before focusing on luxury items. No exceptions! Remember to start the day with the top priorities because you never know what will happen as the day goes on.

Step 5 - Consider not checking email first thing in the morning until a priority is completed. If you can't do that, just respond to critical emails or limit only looking to urgent emails. It's not ideal to spend too much time on the defense responding to emails instead of spending more time being productive working on projects that help you and the organization flourish and increase the bottom line.

Step 6 - Schedule times to check email. Don't just do it randomly all day. If you are curious, track and analyze how many times a day you check email. Also, track how much time you spend reading and answering emails that aren't crucial.

Step 7 - Analyze for time opportunities by charting one full day during the week. Then one full day on the weekend, so you can dig deep and look for opportunities to support your time needs. Every minute must be charted. You might uncover mismanagement of meetings by others, which takes additional time from you. If your meetings routinely go over, that needs to be charted and analyzed. The time traveling to work needs to be charted. If you can carve out a work-from-home day, you would save time traveling to and from work. Would that help? Yes, of course. A few of my clients have done this exercise. It was absolutely stunning what they uncovered. If you can get fifteen or forty-five minutes added to your day to *Win the 16,* that would be fantastic.

Step. 8 - Understand your most creative hours of the day, most productive hours of the day, and best times to schedule meetings or phone calls. Use this analysis to optimize your day–to *Win the 16.*

Step 9 - Learn to say "no" and let others do their jobs as well as take care of their own responsibilities.

Step 10 - Multitasking sounds great, and it's a must for some, but it's not optimal to get your priorities done. Multitasking may get things off our plates, but that doesn't mean it's our highest quality of work. There is increasing data to support that multitasking doesn't deliver the same quality of work compared to someone who is singularly focused on that task. This makes complete sense.

Step 11 - Time management is an on-going process. It's a full-time job every day. Just remember, if you take your eye off it, you will pay the price in different ways, whether it's productivity, additional work, less time doing what you desire, missing priorities and more.

A couple of final thoughts on time management opportunities that could inspire you to view this as an opportunity. If you are a leader, such as a parent, CEO, manager, coach, captain of a team, etc., and you have people who look up to you, please consider this. If you routinely run behind or complain about time issues, does that exude leadership? No, it doesn't. I always want my team to view me as calm, organized and in control. People who don't manage their time well send the wrong message. The average person believes they are swamped and have no time. As leaders, we must be careful not to come across that we are busier, or our time is more important than the person we are talking to.

We control our time. Take accountability for it. If we change our mindset, our time management will be easier. Please don't take this as saying that we don't have obligations that trump our control. We do. The mindset of controlling our time will allow us to spend more time doing what we want.

Takeaways from this chapter include the following:

- Acknowledge time because it's real and can be challenging
- Know your time thieves and distractions
- Learn to say no
- Let others do their jobs and take care of their responsibilities
- Treat our employees like we treat our boss when it comes to time
- Time management is an opportunity, not a negative
- Plan your days and prioritize the critical objectives for that day
- In *Win the 16*, we all have sixteen hours to work with
- *Win the 16* can impact all our lives.

Chapter 14 -
Unforeseen Challenges and Obstacles

Who would like to live in a world where everything you planned for in your day not only happened, but there were no unforeseen challenges? This would be magical. The reality is that challenges and obstacles occur all the time. Climbing Mt. Everest is a daunting task. What makes it even more challenging is you can't control the environment. Action must be based on the situation, not the plan. The environment is ever-changing. Climbing Mt. Everest is not the same as our daily lives, but the insights apply. We can't always control our environment, but the ability to stay calm, use critical thinking and remain focused on our goals is within our reach.

If a family member gets into a critical accident, your day gets turned upside down. All we can do is be the best person, supporter and helper we can be for these types of unforeseen problems. These moments are challenges that must be faced. In *Win the 16,* we want to be proud of our sixteen waking hours. Some days this means taking care of family, friends and your people. As a leader, if my people were distracted due to family issues, I would encourage them to go home and take care of the family. They can come back the next day when they can be fully engaged. One, it is the right thing to do. Two, it is supportive. It allows the employee to go home guilt-free and take care of their family issue. This is an opportunity to lead and show you care about the whole person.

Let's visualize a normal workday, whether that's remote or in person. You are your best self in the mornings. You have a strong agenda for the entire day, intentionally packed with your top priorities scheduled earlier in the day to help ensure you get those done first. The work environment is challenging, but your morning is progressing well. You continue to complete important activities, and then your boss tells you to jump on a call from 11:00 a.m. to 1:30 p.m. Wow! Now you must revamp your entire day. This will sabotage your plan and distract you. In fact, it might be difficult to resurrect the full focus you had prior to the call. This is a real, unforeseen challenge that happens all the time.

To *Win the 16,* we have principles to help us during our sixteen waking hours, such as goals, discipline, and mental toughness. In attempting to *Win the 16,* please remember you might not be able to overcome some unforeseen obstacles. The goal is to manage it all as well as you can, not to fix everything. Below are some steps to help handle unforeseen obstacles and challenges:

1. Taking deep breaths helps decrease stress, relaxes you and improves focus on the situation
2. Develop a positive mindset - Think optimistically and go to a place of happiness for a moment to put all in perspective. This will help you be the best self you can be
3. Ask questions - Seek to understand and receive clarity

4. Figure out how you can help
5. Course correct based on the situation
6. Some situations force us to stop working and care for our loved ones. It's OK
7. Let your core values guide you

When your day is interrupted or your progress stalls, it's easy for your mindset to collapse. You may feel guilty for not following through on your intentions. But you should not feel guilty, and you are human. Seldom do days go perfectly.

Everyone gets distracted. The real divide is between those who get back on track quickly and those who let interruptions expand into longer periods of inactivity. Top performers get back on track faster than most. This is a skill to develop. You will be interrupted, but you can choose to keep it brief.

Takeaways from this chapter include the following:

- The best plans will be interrupted by unforeseen obstacles and challenges
- Course correcting is imperative as our days evolve
- Breathing can help relieve stress in challenging moments
- Top performers get back on track faster than most when they get distracted
- *Win the 16* can impact all our lives

Chapter 15 - Change Agility

Win the 16 is a mindful set of principles to help us optimize our day. The concepts might not be new, but they are also not easy. Living the principles daily is tough without proper guidance and a strategy. It takes thought, planning, discipline, mental toughness and more. To *Win the 16* in our ever-changing world, change agility is imperative in optimizing your day. We must be able to change and adapt so we can grow and evolve.

Win the 16 defines change agility as the ability to modify our behaviors efficiently and effectively in an optimistic way. This aspect of growth mindset is essential. We must buy-in. "Efficiently" is included in this definition because change agility is about change occurring in a timely fashion. We can't wait. The world is moving fast. No matter what business we are in, we must be agile. We discussed the growth mindset concept earlier in the book. We can't afford not to evolve and grow. Optimism ties into this mindset. A positive mindset will help change, especially when the change is hard. Change for some, can be scary and mentally debilitating. It can be helpful if we come to terms with and understand that change is happening every day.

We can't *Win the 16* without acknowledging change is constant and that we need to develop change agility. It's a skill that we can improve. It just takes small steps, but it can happen. Change agility can be practiced. It's in our power to focus on it. Again, it's not easy, just like *Win the 16* isn't easy, but it can be worked on, developed and accomplished. We will see success when we modify our behaviors and make changes in our lives.

There are many positive results when you demonstrate change agility. Usually, when we change or evolve, we learn things. In fact, think of changing as learning. To *Win the 16,* you must be the person equipped to change and learn. You don't want to be the expert of yesterday. Our goal should be for us to be the expert of tomorrow.

This is so powerful. Being an expert on how your world existed last year or even yesterday is just not enough to be our best selves. We need to be the expert of today, tomorrow, and all subsequent tomorrows. This means learning and changing must become a core part of who we are. The world is constantly changing. At times, we endure small changes. At other times we encounter massive changes. Look at what the coronavirus pandemic did to the world in 2020. Learning is pivotal for change agility. We must demand of ourselves to keep learning. Stay optimistic and move forward. People who can do it the most efficiently and effectively will be at a major advantage. The first step in developing a skill is identifying your current level of competence. The next step is to identify where you want to go in developing the skill. Recognizing how difficult change is might help. It can be scary and intimidating. This is where the optimistic mindset and desire to learn can assist us with our change agility. If you can be positive and crave learning, it makes the process a bit easier. The possibilities are endless, and our potential is what we make of it.

As President of Pygon ONE Consulting, I have many different programs for our large, medium or small organizations. We also offer one-on-one coaching for individuals, including executives, directors, managers and sole contributors. Everyday change is paramount in what I do, not only for the people I work with but for me. I must evolve to ensure I meet the needs of those I serve to maximize their potential and customize what we do to assist them in the development and improvements they desire. It is a responsibility that I take on with great pride.

Many years ago, I took my first personality assessment. The assessment changed me. Self-awareness can aid learning and facilitate change. The assessment didn't change my personality, rather, it opened my eyes to who I am. This greater self-awareness helped me understand where I flourish and where I struggle. It provided insight into why I behave the way I do under stress, group settings, competition, and more. It taught me things about myself that I never thought of. It was powerful! The assessment also taught me about other people, as well. It helped me better understand that others aren't bad, they're just different. This helps me more effectively lead and work with others. The assessment made me a better leader, consultant, coach, dad and more. Recently, I did the personality assessment again because we do evolve over time.

How great would it be if you had concepts to optimize your connection and ability to learn and change your behaviors to support your relationships? Why is this part of change agility? Once you learn about yourself, as well as others, you now have more choices to modify your behaviors and change them efficiently and effectively. As leaders, managers, parents and individuals reading this book, you are trying to support people to modify or improve their change agility. Understanding personality types is helpful and allows you to adjust your behaviors and communication in a way that the other person will best respond to. This is the platinum rule of treating people. People want to be treated the way they want to be treated. If we can do that more effectively, it helps us inspire, motivate, communicate and work with others to explore their potential.

My personality type, driver and influencer, embraces change. I enjoy it. Another personality type that we call stable and steady does not love change. They can fight it at times or just ignore it. They are amazing people. They tend to be peacemakers, kind, quality listeners and people you can count on. But they tend to lag in change agility. Another group in the personality assessment, the conscientious, will change, but they must have all the facts and data before they will budge. As a leader directing a group of people, you could give a great speech on why the organization is changing and why we need to adopt change agility. However, if you don't speak to each person individually with a customized approach to meet their own needs, allowing them to get comfortable based on what they need to move forward with this change agility journey, your team as a group collectively could be much slower in meeting the organization's desires.

In closing, there is a man that exemplified change and change agility. He is universal to most, especially here in Chicago. He is Michael Jordan, a former professional basketball player for the Chicago Bulls, a majority stakeholder of the Charlotte Hornets, and a significant stakeholder in his personal Air Jordan brand under Nike. There was no chance, with my being raised in Chicago in the 1980s as well as being a huge fan of his, that Michael Jordan wasn't going to be mentioned in this book. He exuded so many of the *Win the 16* principles.

Jordan's change agility is inspiring. Jordan's Chicago Bulls teams were good, but they could not get past the Detroit Pistons. The Pistons played the Bulls and Jordan ultra-physical after deciding it was the only way to limit Jordan's skill and athleticism. They pounded Jordan, routinely holding, and even knocking him down. After a couple of years of losing in the playoffs to the Pistons and taking this punishment, Jordan knew he had to change. Immediately after the season, he started the journey of getting bigger and stronger. Michael Jordan added fifteen pounds of muscle in one summer to prepare for the following season's games against the Detroit Pistons. His program was so successful that it changed the way athlete's workout and prepare for their seasons to this day. Jordan hadn't lifted weights in the past for fear of ruining his shot, but this off-season, he worked with his trainer, Tim Grover, to increase weight and strength.

Wow! Here you have the best player in the world changing his grueling, disciplined off-season program, one that made him the best player in the world, for an entirely different approach in order to get even better. In real-time, Jordan changed his physique and made his game even better. Please remember, lifting weights like this wasn't routine like it is today. Jordan was hesitant to strength train aggressively because he was already the greatest. The outcome after he adjusted his training was that the Bulls never lost to the Pistons again during the playoffs in the Jordan era. The Bulls went on to win six NBA championships. Jordan continued to evolve as he got older, adding even more to his game. He went from flying to the basket all the time to improving his outside shot. He wanted to remain the best and knew he had to change if he wanted to stay at the top. Jordan won the NBA scoring titles at ages thirty-two, thirty-three and thirty-four. He remains the oldest player to lead the league in scoring and one of only four to do it in their 30's.

Jordan was no longer the greatest athlete as he aged, but he continued to be the best player because he changed and added additional skills. He stayed on top by evolving with the times and his current situation. He didn't try to manage change. He just did it. And in so doing, he continued to soar in the NBA, just in a different way.

Takeaways from this chapter include the following:

- Change agility is a skill and can be worked on
- Change needs to occur in real-time
- Leading people through change or to change themselves requires skill

- Knowing the type of person you are working with during change helps because different personalities need different strategies and support
- To stay at the height of your career, you need to evolve and execute effectively and efficiently
- *Win the 16* can impact all our lives

Chapter 16 - Healthy Lifestyle

Win the 16 is a mindset, philosophy and lifestyle. One of the pillars for living *Win the 16* is a healthy lifestyle. In *Win the 16,* we have agency and choice. Choosing a healthy lifestyle is part of that. Its objective is to improve people's health and well-being by implementing discipline, creating habits and adopting a positive mindset that enables us to be physically and mentally fit, so we can be our best selves.

This chapter is not a lecture on what to eat or how to exercise. It does share ideas on the essence of healthy living and thoughts on living this type of healthy life. For some, this could be a refresher that motivates them to do more. Others may find an opportunity to take that first step in making changes in their life, so they can be their best. *Win the 16* principles are simple but not easy to enact. It's critical to spend time thinking. "How do I engage with *Win the 16* with a mindful purpose and then stay disciplined to implement daily?" Small steps and small goals will help you make these improvements. A healthy lifestyle is a principle in *Win the 16* because we need our mind and body in a place that allows us to maximize our day and potential.

Earlier in the book, we discussed unforeseen challenges. We need energy to work through those challenges because they are mentally draining. Energy is pivotal in the success of our days. Mental challenges, stress, and our own health can zap our energy. Stress is a huge energy thief. It is why the mental piece is just as important as the physical portion of living a healthy lifestyle. Before making any changes to your diet or exercise routine, consult your physician. I view going to the doctor for an annual checkup as getting my report card for the year. How did I do this year? Also, a nutritionist and fitness trainer should be consulted to ensure you make optimal changes. The internet is a double-edged sword. It's incredible for information, but unfortunately, not everything out there is accurate or applicable to you. A doctor, nutritionist and coach are critical to crafting your *Win the 16* healthy lifestyles.

I want to emphasize that living a healthy lifestyle is not about deprivation or subjecting yourself to physical pain. In fact, it's crucial to build a program you enjoy, can sustain, and can help you feel good mentally and physically. There's an abundance of scientific evidence that a healthy lifestyle reduces the risk of cardiovascular disease, strokes, and dementia.

The outline below is to assist you when creating a healthier lifestyle. It should provide a pathway to support your way of life. Here is a step-by-step guide to help you begin the process.

Step 1: MINDSET

A plan for a healthy lifestyle must start with a positive mindset with the expectation it will take some inspiration, goals, discipline, habits, knowledge, preparation, accountability, and mental toughness. Our thoughts on remodeling our lifestyle are consequential. Eliminating sugar from your diet will take discipline and mental toughness. If you attend a work function where pastries and dessert are served, discipline and mental toughness are needed to say, no thank you. This isn't easy. The "win" is how you feel and the exercising of the discipline necessary to abstain from that wonderful cake. Small wins are the key. Life is to enjoy, but a few sacrifices and a plan with the right mindset can make all the difference.

Step 2: GOALS

This will take reflection and time alone to decide what a healthy lifestyle looks like to you. It's imperative you do this. The vision must be yours. You need to know the type of healthy existence you want and what your goals are. This is for everyone—from people who are just beginning to implement a healthy lifestyle to those who are advanced. You must think about where you want this to go. At times, it might be an even bigger challenge for those who are in a solid position with a healthy lifestyle because what you are doing is working. Again, this process is for you. Some people don't know where to start or what is the next step.

A coach, doctor, nutritionist, or health expert can help guide you. Make your goals achievable. Quality sleep is vital to the mind and body, so this could be a goal. Success will breed more success. Small improvements will become bigger over time. Mental health is a major part of a healthy lifestyle. Reducing stress is a problem for many people. Reading for ten minutes a day or going for a walk is a wonderful way to clear our minds. I have just started meditation with a focus on breathing. I am not skilled at either, so it's a challenge. It is frustrating and tough to stay focused on the breathing and relaxation piece. For those that are advanced and doing well on their healthy lifestyle, there are always opportunities to push it to the next level. A coach is especially helpful with new challenges.

Step 3: PLAN AND STRATEGIZE

This is not a cookie-cutter exercise. It is time to create a plan and strategy. You could potentially benefit from a coach, professional advisor, doctor and/or a person knowledgeable about living a healthy lifestyle. Again, if you are just starting out, consult with your doctor to implement a plan. Remember that it starts with one step at a time.

A recurrent theme of *Win the 16* is small steps can lead to large gains. A modest walk every day, a full glass of water first thing in the morning, or simple stretching could improve your journey as long as it's consistent. Mental health and physical health are included in the *Win the* 16 definitions of a healthy lifestyle. For some, pure mental exercises might be your preferred starting point. Your plan could be reading books and doing crossword puzzles.

Step 4: EXECUTION AND ACCOUNTABILITY

Now that a plan and strategy is in place, it's all about execution. The game is on. You have done the preparation and all the set-up work. It's time to enact your plan. To support you, I highly recommend an accountability buddy, friend or coach. It's imperative you have someone to support your *Win the 16*. It must be a person who can encourage you in a way that is productive, especially on days when your motivation is lacking. You also must be able to coach yourself to reach out to your accountability buddy when doubt creeps in. How helpful would it be if you could call or text that person and say, I am not feeling it, and they come to the rescue to help you fight through those doubts?

This is the power of coaches and accountability partners. They help you on the tough days. It's easy to do the work or make sacrifices when you are fully motivated. It's hard when you are not. As I said previously, discipline is when you look in the mirror, and every ounce of your body from head to toe says, "No, I don't want to do that now, I will do it later," but then suddenly discipline jumps in and says, "No, I will do it today, and I will do it now."

Step 5: REFLECTION

You must reflect periodically to ensure your plan is working. It must be doable for you. If it's not, you need to course correct. If you don't, ultimately, frustration will set in, and you will stop. Remember, a course correction could be removing something you will ultimately stop anyway, so figure it out and implement what you could do consistently. It could mean adding to what you are currently doing— more sleep, an additional day of exercise, one less day of exercise, cutting out a hundred calories, reading a little more, more professional development, advancing from stretching to yoga, removing yourself from a stressful environment, avoiding toxic people, no sugar in the coffee and more. The point is you must make sure the strategy is working for you. Some people start a plan they hate, and ultimately, they quit because it's not tolerable.

At times you will struggle, and it will take mental toughness to fight through. Please don't confuse struggling at times with something you deplore. Nothing worthwhile in life comes easy. It is a balancing act, and if it's just miserable, please re-evaluate the strategy and find a potential alternative. Also, this shouldn't be a horrible experience. It may take some discomfort and will take discipline, but the power of a healthier existence to *Win the 16* to maximize your potential is right in front of you, with small steps leading to big results. You can do it!

Step 6: REFRAME GOALS

Once you have accomplished your goals, it's time to reframe them. They don't need to be drastically different, but they need to be tweaked. A healthy lifestyle never stops. You will need to adjust as it's a lifestyle. For those that need help with nutrition, it's not a diet. It's a lifestyle. Most diets don't work long-term. This book is not about diets or eating methods, but I have never felt better and had more energy since I've gone all-in on living a healthy lifestyle. A professional nutritionist, doctor and fitness coach are great choices to assist you no matter where you are currently. Outside perspectives are incredibly powerful and helpful.

Since I was thirty years old, I have wanted to live to one hundred, and I want it to be a quality experience. This means limited or no medications, if possible, energized, functioning mind, mentally and physically fit. This is my true genuine goal. I want to celebrate the kids' retirement parties and their grandkids. Susan and I have a ton of things to do on our "bucket" list.

The goal is achievable, and I can visualize it. Seeing the endpoint helps me do the little things necessary to achieve my goal. A book called "Blue Zones" is about parts of the world that have the most centenarians. It discusses the healthy lifestyle these people live from social interaction, walking everywhere, the amounts of food they consume and more. It's an inspiring and informative read on longevity. I enjoyed it and learned a bunch from it.

Stress can affect sleep, gut health, mood, energy and more. Stress is omnipresent, unfortunately. Controlling or minimizing stress is pivotal in our journey of health. The Zen mindset, breathing exercises, yoga, exercising, and even a brief walk can help us better manage it. Clearing the mind can help us in stressful times. We need to minimize stress as much as possible. It can debilitate our health quickly.

A healthy lifestyle is critical to *Win the 16*. Health is one of my core values. It's a pillar in the book because, to optimize your day, you need to feel good and have energy. As we age, it doesn't get easier, but feeling good is achievable, and it's up to us to make those choices. Living a healthy lifestyle is a challenge for all. Remember, one step at a time will lead to significant gains. We are in this together.

Takeaways from this chapter include the following:

- Sleep is vital to a healthy lifestyle

- Energy is pivotal to optimizing our day
- Mental and physical health are crucial to *Win the 16*
- Small changes and steps lead to big results down the line
- An annual check-up with a medical physician is like receiving a report card
- Consult a doctor when you make changes to your fitness routine or nutrition
- Accountability buddy or coaches can help you
- *Win the 16* can impact all our lives

Chapter 17 – Coaching

Win the 16 defines coaching as assisting, training or guidance from another or self to develop ourselves mentally and physically to be our best selves. Our potential is unlimited, so this development is key, and it can never stop. When I ask clients to choose a word from the above definition that surprises them, they often pick self-coach. It's in the definition because it's a priority to self-coach to *Win the 16.* We will discuss the value of being coached by another person and what to look for from an outside perspective as well as expertise, but we must be able to coach ourselves, no matter what. Self-coaching is pivotal. Your day may be overloaded and stressful. This is when self-coaching must take center stage. We must improve this skill and find a way to be our own best coach when we don't have someone with us.

When you feel stressed, coach yourself to take some deep breaths, breathe and think clearly. Going for a walk outside can help. These are tips to reduce stress. Follow your principles in *Win the 16,* such as mental toughness, mindset, priorities and positivity. Prepare for each day. I plan my day by tackling my largest priorities first. If you complete your most important items first thing in the morning, you will be less stressed if and when things get busier, or obstacles occur in the afternoon. Now, if you deviate from the *Win the 16* time-management concepts of completing top priorities first, you have added to your own stress when unforeseen obstacles and challenges occur. If you can complete many top priorities early in the day, it can reduce potential stress that might arise later. Control what you can control to be your best self as you *Win the 16*.

Self-coaching is important. We coach ourselves all the time. If someone ever asks you, are you a coach? YES. You are. We must be our own best coaches. It all starts with our goal to *Win the 16*. If you think of yourself as a coach and you are coaching yourself as if you were leading someone else, it removes some of the resistance that occurs as we push through unmotivated or tough times. Self-talk can help us accomplish difficult or unpleasant tasks. Again, there is no silver bullet, but it can assist. Self-coaching has similar principles to someone else coaching us.

The following are ways we can self-coach:

- Set crystal clear goals and remind yourself of them constantly
- Create discipline habits to help you through the days when you are unmotivated
- Hold yourself accountable and tell someone your goals, so they can help you
- Optimistic mindset by envisioning yourself completing the daunting task or goal
- Stay positive. Tell yourself you can do this. Focus on your motivations, and you're why to push through the tough days

- Take pride in doing stuff when you don't want to. This can be a very powerful motivation to get through it. Pride is a great feeling
- Celebrate accomplishments, no matter the size, every day

Self-coaching is an advantage when it's utilized consistently and effectively. Our minds are there to protect us. They often help us rationalize not doing something. Self-talk on staying focused on what you need to do can overcome thoughts that rationalize not completing our tasks. It can be so helpful. The goal of this part of the chapter was to equip you with some principles to help you become your best coach. It's much harder than having a coach, but it's critical for your success to *Win the 16*. One self-coaching thought that helps me mentally during challenging moments is to think I will do what most others won't. It's temporary motivation, but it can be a successful tool.

There are many different types of coaches in our world. There are business, life and nutrition coaches, just to name three. I believe in coaching. I am a certified business coach, behavioral consultant and master life coach. They all have a common thread, which is helping people. I believe I can reach my goals more quickly, more effectively and more efficiently with a coach. Life and work can be challenging and complex at times. We all need coaches, but they don't have to be paid positions only. Most of us have people in our lives who have expertise in certain things that can assist us if we ask. Any coaching needs to be consistent.

One-and-done coaching is not optimal. We need consistency, new ideas, different perspectives and courage at times to push through or take the next step. It's imperative that guidance from someone else is steady and regular.

Qualities to look for in a coach are the following:

- Expertise and passion about the subject matter
- Trusting and reliable
- Genuine and honest (we need the TRUTH from our coaches – no matter what it is), I would lose a client before not being truthful. You can't grow without 100% honesty
- Innovative, current, a learner
- Performance and results-driven
- Accountability partner
- Flexible and customized to you (we all need to be coached differently)
- Follow-up and consistent communication
- Inspiring and motivating
- Problem solver
- Simplify complex concepts, tasks, and challenges
- Curious, empathetic, and a listener
- Positive and growth mindset

Brilliant tech leaders found the right coaching valuable. The late Bill Campbell coached many executives in Silicon Valley. He had clients from Google, Facebook, Amazon and others.

Personally, I have a financial and business coach. I look forward to our time together and find it incredibly useful.

Trust, expertise, and honesty are critical in this coaching relationship. I also have non-paid coaches. My brother is a coach for my career and family. Susan, my wife, coaches me on nearly every level. My friend John is my technology advisor and coach on many things. Another friend, Nick, is a coach whether it's advising me on storytelling, marketing for the book and general business.

Certain friends in my life play the role of a coach on many subjects. One key is that no matter who is coaching us, they must be comfortable saying when we are wrong. The second key is that we must listen with an open mind. This doesn't mean we don't challenge it at times. We should because full buy-in is paramount with a coaching relationship. Being an athlete has helped me be coachable. I had to learn to accept criticism. It's part of the job. It made me better. It brought a different perspective.

Our past experiences with coaches and leaders can be lessons we use today to help us *Win the 16*. In eighth grade, I played football for St. Adrian on the south side of Chicago in Marquette Park. In one game, we played against kids from a tough neighborhood who were bigger than us. In that game, we were down by two touchdowns. During a timeout, Coach Reese came onto the field and said, "Boys, they are bigger than you, and they are going to hit you whether you go at them or not, so hit them back and play hard." He threw in a couple of other words I can't share in a book.

The lesson he shared that day is some things are just inevitable. You have a choice: be a victim and endure or fight back. Coach Reese woke us up, got us to control what we could control, and we fought back. We ended up scoring three touchdowns and won the game. It wouldn't have happened without his coaching. He inspired us with a life lesson that can help us all *Win the 16*.

My high school basketball coach, Jim Prunty, was a master of preparation and strategy. Every Monday we watched a film. Tuesday, we knew the player we would be covering and how they played. By Thursday, during the walk-through, it was all reviewed and on Friday night, on the chalkboard before the game was one last check on the strategy. He taught me a valuable lesson on preparation and strategy. Your strategy isn't always going to work, but the preparation is always valuable. This is a life lesson for everything from your daily routines to bigger life goals. Each requires well-thought-out preparation.

In my professional career at ADP, I was a sales representative at twenty-one. One day, my calendar was empty, so I made more than a hundred and fifty cold calls trying to drum up meetings and business. Later that week, Troy Temple, my trainer and mentor, sat me down and told me I needed to manage my time more effectively. Troy shared better ways to employ my days. He combined time management and strategic planning to coach me. Another simple life lesson from a coach that helped me optimize my calendar and day to be more effective. I thought I was doing the right thing; little did I know until Troy showed me. A life lesson that a mentor and coach help.

At Alcon, I had many lessons from coaches that I still use today. Over two decades ago, I was leading a team for the first time. My director was Tom Dooley. He provided excellent coaching advice that I have since shared with many leaders and managers.

Lesson one: Tom told me that I needed to treat people fair but differently because we are different. The second lesson was for me to pick the style of manager and leader I wanted to be, then run with it. He implored me that I couldn't coach and lead people by changing my style based on the performance or the day of the week. I could change my strategy, approach and many other things, but I needed to decide who I was going to be and commit to being that person. People needed to know who I would be and what my style would be. I could not change every day. An inconsistent leader and coach are problematic. It leads to indecision, uncertainty, and insecurity. Tom's suggestion to show up to work with a consistent leadership style was simple but effective.

Shawn O'Neil was a supervisor of mine in the past at Alcon. In my mind, I was ready to get promoted. Shawn and I scheduled a meeting. Shawn was fully present, and when I communicated that I was ready for the next step in my career and shared my performance, the team's performance, the people we were developing, etc., he was very supportive. In fact, he shared more things that were ammunition for me to build my case to get promoted. He made me feel great. Shawn then started naming potential decision-makers and asked about my experience with them. By the end of our discussion, his coaching made me feel great about past and current performance, but he was able to get me to buy-in on what I needed to do to move forward. This situation could have gone much differently and less positively if Shawn didn't lead the way he did. It was an excellent life lesson that coaching can still be a positive experience even when that other person is not getting exactly what they want.

Now, have I had coaches or leaders over the years who were not to the level I would have liked? Yes. One leader didn't genuinely celebrate successes. Instead, they were always worried about the next project or deal. This doesn't inspire or promote good culture. Another example is a leader who was not authentically present and talked incessantly during conversations. Listening and presence are foundations for quality leadership. Learning what not to do is just as important as learning what to do. We can learn something from everyone.

In closing this chapter, my desire was for you to learn some principles that are imperative for you to coach yourself as well as when others coach you and what you should be looking for in a quality coach. This chapter hopefully inspired you to realize you may also have had coaching experiences in your past that could help shed additional light and focus on things that could support your *Win the 16* today. Sometimes we just need to unlock them from our memories. If we focus on our own self-coaching, self-talk and use some outside support from a coach or coaches to understand different perspectives, as well as learn from them and their expertise, the sky is the limit. Untapped potential is awaiting us all. This can assist everyone to *Win the 16* and be our best selves. The pride we can feel will be enormous.

Takeaways from this chapter include the following:

- Self-coaching is fundamental in our progression, development and learning to *Win the 16*
- Self-talk can aid us in challenging times and when motivation is lacking
- Coaches that are inquisitive, experts on the topic, inspire new learnings and keep us accountable make us more efficient and effective
- Reflection of past experiences with coaches and leaders can help our quest to *Win the 16*
- Principles to support self-coaching, coaching and what to look for in a coach
- *Win the 16* can impact all our lives

Chapter 18 – Accountability

Accountability is instrumental to the *Win the 16* program. Let me frame how *Win the 16* views accountability. It is a mindset that I am responsible for my actions, my non-actions, and my decisions. If you decide you are going to start your day with an early success, you must be accountable for that every day. If you are going to add a good habit and delete a bad habit, then you must be accountable. We could go on with every pillar of *Win the 16*, but you see the point, and that is accountability is its own pillar because without it, we can't unlock our potential and become our best selves.

How do we create an accountable culture, given its importance in winning the 16? One way is by admitting fault and taking responsibility. This requires courage, vulnerability and confidence. It's powerful, and people notice.

Accountable people exhibit the following:

- Don't blame others or the situation
- Think in terms of solutions instead of focusing on problems
- Share what went wrong and accept it
- They admit their faults and errors
- They don't blame time. They take responsibility for how they manage time

- Rarely play the victim card

The best way to be accountable as a leader is to make sure you communicate how important accountability is and then back up those words with accountable actions. Setting the expectation that accountability is non-negotiable is critical. This will empower you to lead and increase the opportunity for others to be more responsible for their actions. NO EXCEPTIONS. It's powerful. The relevancy of this to *Win the 16* is that accountability doesn't come and go. It is a lifestyle to be answerable for our actions or non-action. To commit and excel in this area in all parts of our life will help us explore our potential and be our best selves. *Win the 16* demands accountability.

Accountability is hard. Even with the best intentions, we can fall short. A coach or accountability buddy can be helpful. They can hold you accountable in the area you are working on with them. We discussed in the last chapter all the benefits of a coach, and this is another one of them. Your coach or accountability buddy can be someone you text, call, or email who can support you on whatever you need to ensure you are accountable.

Accountability partners need to know they have the power and authority to hold you accountable, so if you try to manipulate or shy away from the commitment, they can say no, you told me to keep you on task. You need to find a way to dig deep and go to a place mentally to get you through this temporary moment that is causing you to contemplate not acting and being unaccountable for what you have committed to. Go do it because you can do it. This is the type of relationship you must create with your accountability partner.

As a leader, manager, coach, accountability buddy, or parent, I would like to change the narrative on holding a person accountable. You are providing a gift when you are holding someone accountable. It isn't easy, but you are genuinely assisting that person on their journey to be their best self. We all need help. Your ability to support that person and keep them on track is a gift to them, even though it might feel uncomfortable. Your strength to keep them moving forward for their goal is a responsibility you agreed to do. It's your duty.

It is important for us to understand the reasons why we don't hold ourselves accountable so that we are aware of situations when this happens to us. Please remember misses can and will happen. The key is to minimize them and be accountable. No Excuses! If it's on us, we admit the miss and take full accountability.

Here are some potential reasons we don't hold ourselves accountable at times.

- Inability to change
- Embarrassed by the results
- Perfectionist (might not want to admit the miss)
- Not committed to the goal
- The project is not a priority
- Worked hard
- Misaligned desires
- Afraid of admitting it and the ramifications

- Easy to blame someone else or a situation instead of taking responsibility

Over the years leading people, it's been critical to improve upon my ability to hold people accountable. It's a skill, so it can be developed. Our ability to hold others accountable can be the difference between success and failure. If we hire people that demonstrate accountability, it increases our chances of meeting and exceeding the organization's objectives. Time spent on this skill for leaders and individuals is well worth the payoff.

Two famous accountable people I find inspiring are Tom Brady, ex-professional football player and future hall of famer, and Jocko Willink, retired United States Navy officer who served as a U.S. Navy SEAL. Both demonstrate the utmost levels of accountability for themselves as well as the teams and people they lead. These men were ultra-successful and exhibited principles of *Win the 16* daily.

Sometimes it's beneficial to read what "good" looks like from people that aren't famous. I have two prime examples of accountability. Kyle Rooney is the first person. He is an excellent businessman and leader. I was fortunate to hire and work with Kyle years ago. Annually at Alcon, we would celebrate the top 10% of the sales team to conclude the year. Kyle was always a good performer, but it's very difficult to win this prestigious award each year. Sitting next to him at the awards ceremony on an occasion that he didn't win was interesting. Kyle's communication at dinner would sound like this. "Next year, I am doing this. I must increase my market share more. I will switch that account. I need to execute my plan." He was incredibly accountable. Kyle and I always joked that the downside of sitting in the seat next to him was that if he didn't win, I had to listen to him all night because he wasn't happy. But it was understandable because he didn't meet his standards of excellence.

The second person I'd like to share a story about is a great friend since college, Mike Fegan. He is a real estate agent. The current environment for selling houses in the Chicagoland area is not good. When I speak to Mike, he takes accountability for what he can do. He doesn't make excuses or focus on the market challenges. The problems are real, but he doesn't use it as a crutch. He accepts it. He is trying to figure out success in this environment. This is accountability! Kyle and Mike are regular people, just like you and me. They have a standard of accountability. They demonstrate and live a life by it.

In closing this chapter on accountability, I will share one small act of accountability that is memorable to me. SPARKS baseball is a youth travel organization in the Chicagoland area. My three boys played for them growing up. Dave Payton was the president. My twins were fortunate to play directly for Dave. The organization had a non-negotiable rule for coaches and players. Everyone in the organization had to shake hands before and after each practice and game. The kids and coaches held each other accountable to ensure this happened. The Sparks were teaching the kids about accountability, habits, discipline, and respect.

Years ago, I went up to Dave and said thank you for teaching my kids how to properly shake hands and for life lessons such as accountability, habits, discipline, and respect. Dave said, thanks. Do you know what else this does? I had no idea. He said it helps the coaches to understand what type of kid they are getting that day. Also, after the game or practice, it allows the coach to recognize the players' performance, encourage the kids if they had a tough day, and say goodbye properly. The Sparks exhibited excellent leadership and coaching. Dave and the organization didn't just talk about the principles of *Win the 16*. They enacted actionable policies to ensure the kids were accountable. I was so impressed that when we later built an AAU basketball organization, we implemented this policy immediately.

Takeaways from this chapter include the following:

- We are accountable for our actions and non-actions
- Accountability buddy and coach will help us be accountable
- Others holding us accountable is a blessing
- Self-accountability is a skill
- Know reasons why we aren't accountable at times, so we can neutralize that moment
- A simple handshake could be a reminder of accountability
- *Win the 16* can impact all our lives

Chapter 19 – Happiness and Future

Why would a chapter link happiness and the future? In *Win the 16*, our daily joy and vision of the future are key determinants. Every day we wake up and work hard for the day's goals, but also with a plan of how the day's actions fit into a broader vision. The routines we create can be demanding, and it can be difficult to balance all the demands on our time. As we noted earlier, time is finite and unforeseen challenges can steal our time from our *Win the 16* priorities.

The concept of the future with winning the sixteen is pivotal. Many of the *Win the 16* principles, such as habits, mental toughness and discipline, will help us achieve our goals today, but many of the achievements are further down the road. Some of our goals could take a week, month, year or longer to achieve. The ability to envision the future is powerful. This sense of purpose can provide us happiness as we lean into the future. If you decide to read a self-help book every morning to learn, start training for a marathon, learn another language or begin a master's program, the benefits you will reap initially are small but will become substantial in the future. It's instrumental we not only envision the future but also find joy in the present. The small achievements need to keep you motivated and engaged.

We have the power and choice to be happy. *Win the 16* believes a life filled with passion, discipline, and purpose will bring joy to you. I live this way. In 2022, I left a well-paying job to start my own business, my own podcast and write this book. The decision was not about the money. It was about a vision, a passion, and a purpose to help other people by sharing how to optimize their day to be their best selves. There is no question that the *Win the 16* mindset and concepts help people immediately if they can commit to and implement them. At Pygon ONE Consulting, we help individuals, leaders, managers and employees in an organization to unequivocally improve themselves, their staff and their organizations. Everyone can benefit and improve, which is what brings me such purpose and joy.

The book and podcast are also fulfilling because they, too, support people on their journey of life. Assisting people in their development and learning is powerful and rewarding. It brings me happiness.

Happiness is important, but it often is secondary to the bottom line. Results are what executive teams, business owners, stockholders, and administrators need on their quarterly and annual reports. While true, could happiness also provide an edge in achieving bottom-line results? There is data available to support that happiness does make a difference. I firmly believe it impacts results. My productivity, patience, creativity, critical thinking, growth mindset and problem-solving is better when I am in a positive, happy mindset. I just don't believe a negative mindset can compete against a person that has a positive mindset. This is why culture is critical to the bottom line.

Unfortunately, some organizations do not focus on it. They spend most of their time on technical skills.

Hopefully, the principles and concepts are being woven together for you. Early successes in our day can cascade to more later. Positivity, mindset, unforeseen challenges, discipline, habits, goals and now happiness play a role in optimizing your day. I can remember taking a happiness course ten years ago. The curriculum resonated with me because it is logical. I am a better husband, dad, son, leader, and businessman when I am happy. Our own joy can increase our opportunity to *Win the 16*.

Here are some ideas to help us all be happy:

- Achieve small goals, wins or successes each day
- Complete a task before the kids wake up or before you check your email
- Write down a couple of things you are thankful for
- Perform a good deed
- Send a nice email or text or handwritten note
- Workout or walk outside first thing in the morning
- Do something kind for someone
- Celebrate your small wins that day
- Write in a journal
- When performing actions, we dislike, visualize the result

Future goals are a part of *Win the 16* because many of the things we do in our daily sixteen hours are intended to achieve future results. It takes a growth mindset to learn, evolve, modify habits and have the discipline to achieve these future goals. Being happy helps us sacrifice today for our future goals. We want employees that take intentional action today, which will benefit their careers two years from now. This vision and future focus can increase an organization's results.

As a career person living the *Win the 16* program, it's imperative our eyes are on the future prize. Our long-term goals need to be devised or at least thought about as we view our impending months and years. A vision is an idea of what we should be striving towards on this expedition. It will take increased expectations and discipline.

Win the 16 isn't about novel concepts, but it does interweave principles that force us to think and dig deep with our thoughts if we want to be our best selves and unleash our unknowable potential.

Takeaways from this chapter include the following:

- Happiness can provide an edge to the individual and company
- People feel good when they do good things for others
- *Win the 16* is not easy, but a positive mindset can assist in unlocking our potential and being our best selves
- Future focus is pivotal in *Win the 16*
- Vision for our future leads to subsequent success
- *Win the 16* can impact all our lives

Chapter 20 - 960

Win the 16 is defined as each day we are faced with sixteen waking hours to conquer. *Win the 16* means taking full advantage of those hours. It means embracing discipline and making choices to achieve victories, no matter how small, throughout the day. Winning is a habit, and successes early in the day can cascade into further successes. Failure and unforeseen moments are sure to happen, but winning the sixteen means course correcting and adjusting your mindset to optimize the moment, being your best self and finishing the day proud.

This chapter is a stand-alone-chapter from time management because of the emphasis on analyzing your day and the charting exercise. It's imperative if we want to add something into our life and we don't have time, we must find it. 960 represents the number of minutes in sixteen hours. I love little kids, and one of the reasons is they view time as infinite. They just have one mode, which is full throttle and go until they drop at the conclusion of the day. As we get older, we all know time is finite. We only have so many minutes in our twenty-four hours to achieve what we need. Some days it can feel like we are just hanging on. Most of us wish we had more time to sleep, work, read, and just do more.

This chapter, 960, is about finding more time for yourself, so you have more time to do what you would like to do. This is an opportunity to uncover some time that could be better used for a larger priority or goal. This should be an exploratory process and a positive mission. Time can be elusive. You might discover certain phone calls or meetings are longer than you thought, and it's something that could be modified. Social media and email are more activities that eat away at our time.

Analyzing your 960 minutes in the day should be straightforward. Identify all the items that consume time, including emails, meals, meetings, calls, texts, parenting time, problem-solving, managing other people's problems, school, transportation, interruptions, social media, walking, working out, supervisor communication, direct reports, kids and more. Anything that takes up time in your *Win the 16*. Then document your current priorities and things you'd like to add to your day or week. These two lists direct you to apply the time appropriately and channel it toward your priorities.

You probably can anticipate where this activity is going. If you chart your day from the time, you rise until you go to bed, you now have data to work with on potentially adding something to your day. Reminder, before you start tracking your day, it's important you write down your priorities and things you would like to add to your days. This will support you as you chart your day. By charting your day, you will be even more effective in winning the 16, and it will help you to reach your goals whether time management is a strength or not. Remember, time can be elusive. For those that struggle with time management, this could be a game-changer. To get started, pick a day during your week. Optimally, one day on the weekend as well. The charting of your time must be precise, so the data is accurate. Below is a chart for you to do this initial exploratory analysis. However, you track your day, that tool must be with you at your side the entire day, so you can document every minute. Below is an example to illustrate it for you. Lastly, I am not telling you exactly when to sleep. This is just a generic example assuming you sleep eight hours.

** 10:00 p.m. to 6:00 a.m. SLEEP

6:00 a.m._____6:15 a.m._____6:30 a.m.
_____

6:45 a.m._____7:00 a.m._____7:15 a.m.
_____

7:30 a.m._____7:45 a.m._____8:00 a.m.
_____

8:15 a.m._____8:30 a.m._____8:45 a.m.
_____

9:00 a.m._____9:15 a.m._____9:30 a.m.
_____

9:45 a.m._____10:00 a.m._____10:15 a.m.
_____

10:30 a.m._____10:45 a.m._____11:00 a.m.
_____

11:15 a.m._____11:30 a.m._____11:45 a.m.

12:00 p.m._____12:15 p.m._____12:30 p.m.

12:45 p.m._____1:00 p.m. _____1:15 p.m.

1:30 p.m._____1:45 p.m. _____2:00 p.m.

2:15 p.m._____2:30 p.m. _____2:45 p.m.

3:00 p.m. _____ 3:15 p.m. _____3:30 p.m.

3:45 p.m. _____4:00 p.m. _____4:15 p.m.

4:30 p.m._____ 4:45 p.m. _____5:00 p.m.

5:15 p.m. _____5:30 p.m. _____5:45 p.m.

6:00 p.m. _____6:15 p.m. _____6:30 p.m.

6:45 p.m. _____7:00 p.m. _____7:15 p.m.

7:30 p.m. _____7:45 p.m._____8:00 p.m.

8:15 p.m. _____ 8:30 p.m. _____ 8:45 p.m.

9:00 p.m. _____ 9:15 p.m. _____ 9:30 p.m.

9:45 p.m. _____ 10:00 p.m.

Good luck with your analysis and your exploration of where you can find additional time in your 960 minutes to maximize your *Win the 16*.

Takeaways from this chapter include the following:

- There are 960 minutes in sixteen hours
- Time is critical in *Win the 16*
- Everyone wants more time in our days
- Analysis of the current management of your time is not negative, and it's a positive mission
- Time is elusive
- Chart every minute and hour of a day during the week and one day on the weekend
- The charting process supplies precise data to uncover opportunities for additional time
- *Win the 16* can impact all our lives

Chapter 21 - Mission Plan

We have completed our time together learning and understanding the principles and concepts of *Win the 16* as well as the philosophy and mindset behind it. The goal is to wake up every day with the belief that you will *Win the 16*. An objective without a plan, discipline, habits, mental toughness, positivity, growth mindset, change agility, awareness of unforeseen obstacles and accountability is more like hope rather than an authentic deliverable. It is not a strategy. At this point, it's in your hands to develop your *Win the 16*-mission plan with your coach, accountability buddy, or whoever makes sense to assist in your plan and support your efforts.

I have developed a template for you to complete to serve as a guide on your voyage. Please invest in your present and future with this format. The amount of time you spend with earnest contemplation and authenticity will enable you to put forth an astounding *Win the 16*-mission plan. It's pivotal you take time by yourself to carefully consider your mission plan. The potential to positively impact your sixteen waking hours is possible. You can do this!

Win the 16 Mission Plan

Complete the categories below after you have carefully considered each item. What are your motivators? What inspires you? What will be your early successes in the day? This could change during your week. What are your real goals, personally and professionally? Which habits will be added or deleted from your life? Document your healthy lifestyle adoptions and subtractions. An accountability buddy and coach will be important choices. Pick the day to identify time management opportunities to open additional time. All of this will take thought, discipline, a positive mindset, mental toughness, change agility, time, self-coaching, self-talk and a partner to help on the journey.

Remember, you will encounter unforeseen obstacles. Your normal busy life will attempt to impede you from creating your genuine, well-thought-out mission plan. Don't let the chatter in your head stop you. Make the time investment to put together a mission plan. This could be a game-changer and a point in your life when you look back and say, I remember the moment I developed a strategy and planned to become my best self.

Lastly, this is just an example template to guide you. If it's easier for you, do it in your preferred digital format.

*TIP - Ensure you choose small goals and larger goals. Don't overdo it. Small steps! It's critical you have some early successes. We need that sense of accomplishment when making adaptations to our lives. You need to feel good about what you are doing. Small wins will lead to more wins. This won't be easy, but you can do it with deep thought and discipline. We are in this together!

Motivators:

_____
_____
_____
_____
_____

Inspiration:

_____
_____
_____
_____
_____

Early Success in the day:

_____
_____
_____
_____
_____

Goals:

_____
_____
_____

Habits:

Time management (uncover):

Healthy lifestyle adoptions or subtractions:

Accountability buddy:

Coach:

Chapter 22 - Your Greatest 365

The last chapter provided the template for your mission plan for *Win the 16*. This section on "your greatest 365" is a stretch assignment. Once you have completed your mission plan for *Win the 16*, and are making progress and consistently winning your sixteen hours, consider investing in your greatest 365. This is a thought experiment crafting your optimal greatest 365. Your greatest 365 is based on the number of days in a year. The task is much like the *Win the 16*, except now you are crafting what your best year would be. This is not a quick and easy ask. It should be like *Win the 16* in terms of thought process. It's imperative to think and dig deep into your thoughts of what your great 365 would look like.

This is a contemplative assignment for you to take on. It's critical a coach or accountability buddy works with you on this as you go through it. You need help on this one. They will need to be able to ask you questions about your vision, encourage you to push farther or even help you look at your vision realistically and objectively. It's not a journey you should take by yourself because if you do, you might not reach or uncover your greatest 365. Another perspective is critical to support and even challenge you on this assignment. Again, this could be a game-changing moment for you.

Discussions with numerous coaches led to a game-changing moment for me. I told myself many times I wasn't going to write a book at this point when I was going through my greatest life. Mark Lucas, a trusted friend and excellent leader as well as coach, questioned me on the book writing. By the time we hung up the phone, I had another view on it. He helped me to explore it more. My friend, Jen Kobes, pushed me. Many questioned me on the book. I would not be at this point without all of them.

To assist you with areas to explore when you initiate your greatest 365 expeditions, here are some topics to discuss with your coaches as you devise the greatest year:

- What is your why and purpose
- Who, what, and how are you inspired
- What's your vision of your future
- What are critical things of importance
- How do family and friends fit into your life
- What is your health status
- How important is money
- What is your career satisfaction
- Define your current role vs. dream role vs. potential role
- What makes you happy
- What pride do you take in your current 365
- Where do you want to live
- Who do you want to spend your time with
- What are you willing to sacrifice to make for your greatest 365

- What is your risk
- What is your change agility (real-time change)
- What do you do for personal and professional development and fulfillment
- Who is your support team
- What do you want to stop doing
- What is it you have always wanted to do
- What are your core values
- What are your passions
- What are your strengths and weaknesses

This chapter should assist in discovering your greatest 365. It can unlock thoughts you didn't know you had and take you to places you might not have dreamed about or considered. This is your greatest 365. What might start out as a strange, challenging assignment will eventually assist you in clarifying the greatest year of your life?

Hopefully, your mindset is shifting to nothing can stop me! If I didn't dream, plan, take a risk and more I would never have started my own business, Pygon ONE Consulting, write a book, create a podcast and host it with my brother, Bud, all in the same year. I share this because most wonderful things do not happen without dreams, contemplative plans, strategy, goals, optimism, effort, coaching, discipline, challenges, risk, trepidation, change agility, and inspiration.

You can do it. You just need some guidance and support to accelerate this opportunity of a lifetime. Everyone's view of excellence is different. It's a process. If you take on this task to explore what your best 365 would look like, I am sure it's going to be time well invested in your future. You might uncover you are already living the greatest 365. Amazing!

Takeaways from this chapter include the following:

- Thinking and deep thought are critical to explore your greatest 365
- Time will be needed to explore what is your greatest 365
- A coach or accountability partner needs to go on this journey with you to assist you in crafting your best 365
- *Win the 16* can impact all our lives

Chapter 23 - Final Thoughts

The hope of *Win the 16* is to provide a daily strategic game plan to guide your personal and professional life. Optimizing our day is never easy, and it absolutely requires a certain mindset. This is a lifestyle and philosophy on how to live our days to the fullest. If you focus on making modifications, no matter how small, it places you in a better position to win your sixteen and be your best selves. The concepts in this book will help you explore your potential and ultimately allow you to go to bed at night, being proud of your day. The growth mindset we discussed focuses on learning and development. Again, if we can focus on progression and knowledge rather than speed or outcome, our long-term success can skyrocket to new heights. Small steps in our own personal and professional advancement will lead to larger successes in the future. Remember to celebrate small and large wins.

In conclusion, you have just taken yourself through *Win the 16* strategies through your own optics. This should help you process what genuinely resonates with you. This is the first step in implementing sustainable change. Use your mission plan as a tool to guide your strategy. Our lives continue to move very quickly. No better time than today to start winning the sixteen.

I implore you not to speed through the process. The more quality thought and time you put into what you desire will ultimately drive your success with your own *Win the 16*. This is your life and your sixteen hours to be your best, live it with great pride. It's all right to be scared or nervous about making changes in your life. In fact, it is healthy and normal. The key is not to allow those feelings to stop you. Failure is not an option because no matter what you do, you are pushing yourself to grow and increase the opportunity of getting closer to maximizing your potential.

An accountability partner or coach should be brought in early during this process, so you can share thoughts and ideas about *Win the 16*. They can help you set your path and provide valuable perspective. In this book, we discussed how so many coaches in our lives helped us grow and how accountability partners are helpful in supporting us, identifying blind spots, and course correcting. As a reminder, the following concepts are pillars to *Win the 16*:

- Motivators and inspiration
- Mindset and positivity
- Mental toughness and discipline
- Early successes to your day
- Goals and habits
- Time management and 960
- Unforeseen challenges and obstacles
- Coaching and accountability partner
- Accountability
- Healthy lifestyle
- Happiness and future

All the best on your journey in winning your 16! You can live this lifestyle daily. It will take your commitment, discipline, time, deep thought and accountability to complete and execute your mission plan once you create it.

Just remember, small steps every day will have major results in the future. The effort and time pledged spent on *Win the 16* will propel you to even greater accomplishments and more enjoyment in your life. Our best selves are achievable. We can do it! Good luck to all!

Appreciation

Thank you for allowing me into your life for a short period of time to read *Win the 16*! The book writing experience has enabled me to grow in areas I didn't know were possible. I hope you, the reader, have enjoyed the book as much as I did writing it. It was an unforgettable experience.

Thank you to those that contributed to this book. Special appreciation to Kerry, Susan, Bud, AP, Nick, and John. I would not have this final product without you. Your teachings, insights, coaching, and expertise were invaluable.

Thank you to my family and friends for the support and guidance during this writing journey.

Thank you to the leaders, coaches, supervisors, peers, direct reports, clients and teachers who have impacted my professional and personal development.

Thank you to Automatic Data Processing, Alcon Laboratories, and Novartis for the development and support during my professional career.

Thank you to Erica, Mike, and the Genesis Barbell community for the support in living a healthy lifestyle.

Thank you to the clients at Pygon ONE Consulting for sharing your knowledge and expertise.

About Pygon ONE Consulting

We are a small business that believes people are core to an organization's success. Our mission is to support an organization's full potential of their people and performance in this complex and competitive environment.

Pygon ONE Consulting provides the following services:

- Leadership and management development
- *"Win the 16"* inspirational talk and instructional training program
- Executive coaching and individual contributor coaching for groups and one-on-one
- Enrich employee engagement for remote and hybrid workers

*All services provided in-person and virtual

You are invited to learn more about Pygon ONE Consulting at our website, pygonone.com. Please contact us for any questions or to seek information about potential interests. Lastly, you can listen to the "Win the 16" podcast on most major platforms.

Pygon ONE Consulting

Website: pygonone.com

Email: Dpygon@pygonone.com

Headquartered: Chicago, Illinois

USA and global work offered